I Believe in the Living God

Books by
Emil Brunner

Published by The Westminster Press

I Believe in the Living God

The Letter to the Romans

Faith, Hope, and Love

The Great Invitation, and Other Sermons

Eternal Hope

The Misunderstanding of the Church

The Christian Doctrine of Creation and
Redemption, *Dogmatics, Vol. II*

The Scandal of Christianity

The Christian Doctrine of God, *Dogmatics, Vol. I*

Man in Revolt

The Mediator

The Divine Imperative

Revelation and Reason

I BELIEVE IN THE LIVING GOD

SERMONS
ON
THE
APOSTLES'
CREED

BY

EMIL BRUNNER

TRANSLATED AND EDITED BY

JOHN HOLDEN

Philadelphia
THE WESTMINSTER PRESS

CONTENTS

TRANSLATOR'S NOTE

I FIRST MET Emil Brunner in the fall of 1947 when I enrolled as a student at the University of Zurich. That year he was offering courses of instruction in systematic theology and homiletics, a fact indicative of his ability as both a profound Christian thinker and a popular city preacher. Brunner has not only gone down in church history as one of the most outstanding Protestant theologians since the Reformation; he has also paved the way in the communication of the gospel to modern man. His book of sermons entitled *The Great Invitation* already has influenced pulpits throughout the church in this country. And those who know something about contemporary preaching on the Continent can recognize Brunner's influence there. Yet I do not wish to idolize any preacher; I do wish to take this opportunity to thank God that he has given us a man who can both think and preach.

Many of us are familiar with the larger technical works by Brunner in the field of theology, but we know little about the way he applies his theology in the field of preaching. Because the dialectical theology came to America from Europe (I see no reason why we should not admit this!) in the form of massive volumes of theology, it has thrived primarily on university and seminary campuses but has run into some difficulty when it has tried to penetrate the parish. As a seminary student I often heard fellow Princetonians remark after almost any course that required us to read one or more books by Brunner, "I wish one could preach this theology." Perhaps this book of sermons on the Apostles' Creed in its English translation will help meet this need and promote somewhat better relations between theology and homiletics than existed in my days at the seminary. I hope that it encourages someone to explore further the questions on the boundary between theology and homiletics. Here a great service could be rendered to the church in America.

Some who read this book may not be familiar with Brunner the theologian. They will find it a most valuable introduction to the main doctrines of the Christian faith presented in language they can understand. In these sermons, the Apostles' Creed, which we repeat, sometimes mechanically, at Sunday morning worship, comes alive and shocks us with its relevance to problems all of us face: anxiety, guilt, doubt, suffering, and death. After one has listened to these sermons he feels like singing the Apostles' Creed as believers once sang it during the days of the Reformation. It may also happen that this exposition of the creed will inspire some to dig deeper into the meaning of their faith and thereby encourage a much-needed dialogue between the laity and the theologians of the church. But let me make one thing clear. I did not translate these sermons so that they could be used primarily as a study booklet in some comfortable church group or as an interesting specimen of current ideas. I translated them because I trust that through them God may speak his word of judgment and promise to us.

These sermons were preached originally during the Second World War, and some dated material that might have distracted the reader today has been removed at the suggestion of the publisher. Brunner agreed to this suggestion and co-operated fully with me in this slight revision of the sermons as originally published in German. I wish to thank both the author and the publishers' staff for all the kind, patient assistance they have given me.

JOHN HOLDEN

PREFACE

THESE SERMONS, LIKE the ones already published in English, were preached in the Fraumünsterkirche, Zurich. Although their Biblical texts are timeless, that is, true in all times and under all circumstances, it is my conviction that in order to reach the heart and mind of the present-day reader they must be interpreted in such a way that our time—this time of anxiety and apprehensions—must be reflected in them.

It is necessary that we be placed upon firm ground that does not waver even if the whole world is shaken at its foundation. In this age, when the bond between the nations of Christendom is so lamentably disrupted, it seems to me doubly neecssary to remind ourselves of the common creed of the Christian churches. It is usually called the Apostles' Creed. Those versed in history tell us that it does not stem from the apostles but was composed in the first centuries after Christ. Even so, it is still a truly common expression of early Christendom and can therefore be valid as the confession of our faith in God the Father, the Son, and the Holy Spirit.

Its great merit is that it points to the basic facts of the life of Christ; its main weakness is that it does not speak of these facts as the apostles did, namely, as facts that only those who believe in Jesus Christ can know and of which only they can understand the meaning. In this sense, however, the Christian faith remains bound to it, and we like to use it as the shortest catechism of Christianity. This creed runs:

> I believe in God the Father Almighty, Maker of heaven and earth;
>
> And in Jesus Christ his only Son our Lord; who was conceived by the Holy Ghost, born of the Virgin Mary, suffered under Pontius Pilate, was crucified, dead, and buried; he descended into hell; the third day he rose again from the dead; he ascended into heaven, and sitteth on the right hand of God the Father Almighty; from thence he shall come to judge the quick and the dead.
>
> I believe in the Holy Ghost; the holy catholic church; the communion of saints; the forgiveness of sins; the resurrection of the body; and the life everlasting. Amen.

For the theologians who raise the question, How far are we bound by it, how far not, and in what sense is it imperfect? my last volume of *Dogmatics,* which is soon to appear, tries to give an answer. But the average layman, who does not ask this question as much as he tries to hear through it the word of God himself, may be grateful for an interpretation that takes account of the difference between the working of our minds and that of the minds of the first centuries. Nothing is truly accomplished by regarding all that is said in the Bible or in the creed as true. True Christian faith is not "to believe something," but to trust and obey the One who speaks to us in the Bible and through the creed, with our whole heart.

It is the intention of these twelve sermons to show in what sense faith in Jesus Christ includes the facts to which the creed refers and to show what this belief means in our life, both individually and socially.

May they lead many to that living faith in Jesus Christ, or strengthen and clarify it, and by so doing help to build his body as the light of the world and the salt of the earth within this generation, misled by illusions or beginning to doubt all meaning in life.

EMIL BRUNNER

Zurich, July, 1959

I God
the Creator

I believe in God the Father Almighty,
Maker of heaven and earth.

In the beginning God created the heavens and the earth.
(Gen. 1:1.)

He is the image of the invisible God, the first-born of all
creation; for in him all things were created, in heaven and
on earth, visible and invisible, whether thrones or dominions
or principalities or authorities—all things were created through
him and for him. He is before all things, and in him all things
hold together. (Col. 1:15-17.)

YOU ARE PERHAPS a little astonished that I am
beginning this series of sermons on the Christian
creed and have chosen for today a text so timeless
and remote, when all our thoughts are imprisoned in
the threatening events of these days. I owe you an

explanation. First, it should be said that precisely in these days nothing is so important as this, that we stand fast in the faith. The storm has not yet reached us; we have received only a small wind from its periphery. The really difficult times may still lie before us; they will be difficult even if we ourselves remain exempt from conflict; they would be dreadfully difficult if we should be drawn into it. Either way, not only our economic but also our spiritual reserves, and above all our reserves of faith and love, will be required. We must lay up reserves of faith. That means we will have to do everything in these days to strengthen ourselves out of God's Word and in prayer for the coming difficulties, to create, to collect heavenly treasures, so that we can hold out and do not fail in the days of greatest scarcity. As a soldier receives provisions before combat and checks whether he has everything that belongs to his equipment, so we also want to examine and obtain the equipment of our faith so that we have it when the need comes. We should, indeed, always do that; it is true of all days and even of so-called normal times that we do not live by bread alone but by every word from the mouth of God. But now we understand better than before how urgently necessary that is, how much faith is a question of existence, no, is in the last final *the* question of existence. This struggle is, indeed, really a war of faith. It is concerned not only with power and economic goods; rather, it is concerned with whether the proclamation of God's Word shall remain free, or whether Christendom and the Christian congregation must again crawl into the catacombs because the powers on earth are enemies of Christendom and all faith in God. There can also come again for the church times of hunger when one may preach, read the Bible, and pray together only in hiding places. Therefore, work while it is still day!

The second thing is this, that we, precisely when we reflect upon the ultimate questions of our faith, should come to the realization that at any time and also now they are the most contemporary. There drops from every one of the great words of the Bible a particularly clear light upon the events of time. We can understand what the issues are today only when we place ourselves at the highest height. We can recognize what God requires of us today and what he especially gives us today only when we reflect upon the deepest foundations of our faith. He who wants to build a solid house must lay his foundation deep. Superficial things, of which there are indeed enough, will not really be of service to us today. We want to build our house upon rock, upon God's own Word, upon Jesus Christ, and everything that can make God's Word great to us and Jesus Christ the center of our thinking and willing; that and that alone is now truly relevant to the times.

So we want to allow God's Word to speak to us today what it says about the creation and the Creator. The Old Testament begins with what is the beginning of all things. As the Word of the Creator is the beginning of all things, so it should also be the beginning and foundation of our faith. But so we may know from the outset who the Creator is and where we can best recognize him, the New Testament tells us that this Creator is none other than the God who has disclosed his nature and his will in Jesus Christ. God the Creator and God the Redeemer are one. The Son of God, who is the eternal Word of God, is the personal plan of creation, the divine model of creation or the goal of creation. The beginning and the end of all things belong together. We can understand whither we are going only if we understand whence we have come, and we can understand whence we have come only if we understand whither we are going. The architect has a blueprint before he undertakes the construction. The goal lies before him before he allows the first spade to break ground. In God the beginning and the end are one. In this blueprint of God, which is Jesus Christ and the Kingdom of God, we are included, every one of us. As God has a blueprint for the whole world, so he also has a blueprint for our life as part of the great plan. Our beginning and our destiny are in the hand of God.

Is it not something enormous to dare to believe that today? What so frightens us today is that godless powers are running wild. It seems as if everything has become meaningless. Everything that is worth-while, everything for which we have worked, everything that has taken mankind thousands of years to build up, seems at present to be threatened. Nothing is left standing firm, and the end again seems to be nothingness, a life that is no longer worth living. Over against all this God now says to us in his Word: No, it is not so. What seems to be important from the viewpoint of the world is really not important. The great events of the world that frighten you are really not the final events. The present is not your destiny but only a hammer blow in God's great construction. You see only the foreground, which is terrifying. Keep your eye on the background, which is divine. The foreground is really small in comparison with the background, but it always seems larger to us because it is in front. To believe is to see the world's background. The faith of creation that the Word of God proclaims to us is this: behold the foundation of everything, and behold it in Jesus Christ, the Son of God, the plan of the world. And then, if you really see that, you will no longer be frightened and no longer despair. Then you have faith.

And what do we need today more than faith? That solid faith that everything will still turn out well. We as Christians who believe in the Word of God have a proud and divinely rooted optimism. We know because God has spoken to us that, although the great world powers would like to do whatever they please, God has control of all of them, that even when they think that they are making world history they are still nothing else than small chessmen who must move as God shifts them, that still in spite of all sorts of catastrophes God's world plan still goes on.

But what is the goal? the end? It is by the mercy of God that he has revealed to us the goal and end of everything as plainly as the beginning. The beginning of all things is: God spoke and it was. It was a slow development over billions of years, but it was at his bidding. And the end is: it will be, though through long historical developments, through countless catastrophes and new beginnings, but it will be: his Kingdom. For all that is created is created in him the Son. He is the divine design; he is the meaning of everything; he is the ultimate purpose and final goal of everything that happens.

Let us say it in a more personal way. God created man in his image. He created you and me to be like him, to be the mirror of his spirit, his love. The more you allow God to look upon you and in you, the more like him you become. God looks at you in Jesus Christ, and when you allow yourself to be seen by God in Jesus Christ you become like him. That is God's grace, that he looks at you and me in Jesus Christ, that he does not say to us, as we sometimes say to a man or at least think: I do not care to see you. That is his whole love, his mercy, his forgiveness. But it is also his will to perfect us, to cleanse us of all evil and to place his Holy Spirit in us. God's view, God's looking at us, is a creative looking. He wills that we at the appearance of Jesus Christ become like him. That is his building plan for you and me. Every man can reach the destiny of his creation, and that means his true humanity, only if he becomes like

God, the image according to which he was created and the original image of which is Jesus Christ. And he can reach this likeness with God only if he allows himself to be seen by God in Jesus Christ. That is our Christian world outlook. It is no world outlook that we make; rather, it is God's looking at us and our looking at God in Jesus Christ.

In Jesus Christ we see two things: God the Father and ourselves as God wills to have us. That is the mystery of Jesus Christ, that he reveals to us these two things. He is therefore the first-born of all creatures. He is the goal of God's creation and he is at the same time the goal of our lives, the true God and the true man in one, the God-Man. We ought to be like him.

But we know that we are not what God created us to be, and we know why: because we do not allow God to look at us and do not allow ourselves to look at him; because we are always making our own views; because we live according to our own views; because we also have other views of ourselves and of our fellow men, and allow ourselves to be determined more by them than by the contemplation of God. We are other than what God wills to have us because we become godless through this looking away from God. With a mirror the important thing is what it reflects. The image in the mirror is not really in the mirror itself; it is outside the mirror. But the image in it is according to what it reflects. So we are. We are no longer God's images because we do not reflect God's face. What, then, do we reflect? One can say: we reflect the world, and we reflect ourselves. Instead of living by looking at God, we live by our world views. And instead of loving God who looks at us in love, we love ourselves. We thereby make the world and ourselves gods. We do that every day a number of times, even though in small ways and without knowing what is going on. Again and again we are in love with ourselves and the world instead of loving God with our whole heart. And from this self-love and world-love comes all evil. From it comes also all the terrible godlessness that we are experiencing at present. God is abolished; and man, his race, his nation, his power, his reason, and his economic system have been made gods. This godlessness is in the midst of us. But do not forget that it is also our godlessness. The present world crisis is the result of a long slow process of blood poisoning of the world. And there is no one who has not contributed his little drop of poison to it. These little drops of poison form a poisonous stream that then poisons the whole world anew. It is true that we will find the poison of godlessness concentrated in certain specific places, but this poison has come from the whole world, even from you and me. We also have contributed to the total godlessness that has come upon us today.

Is there, then, nothing that can be done? Is it simply that man is just perverted and remains perverted and therefore must again and again go to his own ruin? If there were nothing that could be done, then

there would be no sense in preaching. It is just because there is something that can be done that there
is a church, a Christianity, a Bible, and prayer. And
there is something that can be done because God has
done something. He does not allow man to turn away
from him. He has come extra close to us so we can no
longer shun him. But he has come in order to look
at us again and so we may look at him again. That is
Jesus Christ. In him the image of God and therefore
also the true Man has once again become visible to
us. Now we can see God again just as he can see us.
And in him who now sees God again something new
takes place. The godlessness vanishes, and the image
of God comes forth. The creation is restored. The
goal of creation for man is not yet perfected but the
goal begins to be seen. The image of God appears
when we allow Jesus Christ to have an influence upon
us. To let Jesus Christ influence us is what the Bible
calls faith. We should allow Jesus Christ to cleanse us
of evil and to place the love of God in us.

How does that actually take place? It happens as
God wills it, right now in listening to the sermon.
It happens also when one with faith allows the word
of God to speak to him through the Holy Scriptures.
It happens when we allow what we have read to move
our hearts just as the photographer moves the fluid
over the plate until the picture comes forth. It happens when we lay everything we experience before
God in prayer so he may bless or cleanse it. It happens
when we take the time to allow God to speak to us

and when we take the time to speak to him.

It also happens when we take the trouble to love our neighbor as Christ loves us, as God loves us in Jesus Christ. That we forgive those against whom we bear some grudge, that we love those who have in some way made it difficult for us, that we do not condemn one who goes some particular way that we may think is completely wrong and would not take ourselves. That we are, above all, there when he needs us, that we take the trouble to discover where a hidden need is, where there is one waiting for us, where there is one who needs a friendly word and a helping hand from us.

But how does all this alter world events? It changes things first of all because there is then at least one place in God's creation that is not destroyed but is preserved as it should be. Life has meaning. For what is it that gives meaning to life if not humanity? And what is the origin of love if not the love of God for us? Wherever that takes place, there is what is right. And where that happens, it is like a light in the dark, a fire in the cold world, an oasis in the desert of godlessness and of destruction. This oasis can be larger or smaller. It can be only as large as your house, or it can be as large as your neighborhood or your city. Or there may be so many oases in our city and in our nation that they will give the vision to the whole city and even to the whole nation. That is the meaning of the Christian life. Even today. We do not know how many oases will be left after we have passed through these critical years. But we do know that the goal of God's creation is coming forth wherever there is one, that there life is running along the pathway of the divine creation. And above all we know that even all of the evil and godlessness of men cannot hinder God from perfecting his work of creation. The great godless powers of our time can no more hinder God's purpose than could Judas and Pilate and Caiaphas. Even they must unwittingly serve him. And that is why we, as those who know that, will therefore remain cheerful and joyful in the midst of all the catastrophes and tragedies that may come our way. It is only the foreground; the background is God's work of creation, whose plan and purpose we know in Jesus Christ our Lord. Amen.

II   The Father Almighty

I believe in God the Father Almighty,
Maker of heaven and earth.

*I am the Lord, and there is no other. . . . I form light and
create darkness, I make weal and create woe, I am the Lord,
who do all these things.* (Isa. 45:5, 7.)

*See what love the Father has given us, that we should be
called children of God; and so we are.* (I John 3:1.)

IN THE FIRST sentence of the Apostles' Creed,
which we wish to consider once again today, an expression is used that cannot be found anywhere in the
Bible: "the Father Almighty." The Holy Scriptures
teach both that God is almighty and that he is the
Father. It may or may not be an accident that this
expression, "the Father Almighty," cannot be found

anywhere in the whole Bible. This much is certain: we do find it difficult to keep both things in mind at the same time—the almightiness of God and the fatherly love of God. We shiver when we hear the powerful word of Isaiah: "I am the Lord, and there is no other. I form light and create darkness, I make weal and create woe, I am the Lord, who do all these things." It is as if this word must strike us to the ground, as if our breath were knocked out of us. The majesty and almightiness of God cannot be more strikingly expressed than it is in this word of God in The Book of Isaiah. But then the question arises in our minds: Is that the same God of which John speaks, "See what love the Father has given us, that we should be called children of God; and so we are"? When we hear that, our heart expands and begins to rejoice within us; the stricken man stands up not on his own power or self-trust but by the hand of God which comforts us. Are both things true, that which Isaiah says and that which John says, or is it perhaps so that the one is Old Testament and therefore, so to speak, obsolete, superseded by the New Testament, and that the other is New Testament proper and therefore normative for us? It is of the greatest importance that we find a clear answer to this question.

For it is indeed a question that not only the Bible but also contemporary reality forces upon us. But here the case is just the opposite. If we look at reality, at the world over which the black handkerchief of mourning is spread, at this world in which the individual man no longer counts, in which life is extinguished as one snuffs out a candlelight with two fingers—we can still in any case conceive of a majestic, almighty God but in no case of a God of fatherly love. There are at present many thousands, even millions, and there will be even more who in moments of great despair raise the qustion: Where is the God of love? Can there really be a Father looking on when it goes so with his children? Can a Father permit his children to ruin the lives of one another so much? Can a kind, loving Father allow so many innocent people to suffer, to suffer often more terribly than anybody else? And if even we who are still more or less looking on and are only slightly involved find this question a tormenting one, how much more must it burn and agitate in the hearts of those who are most directly involved in this suffering. How must it be, for example, for mothers to have courage who are now without a roof over their heads, without heat, without food at the beginning of a severe winter, their husbands and brothers and sons dead, and some crying, freezing, hungry little children to whom they can give neither bread nor warmth? With what passion their question must rise to heaven: Where are you, God, of whom they have taught us that you are a loving Father? One can well understand why many sober-minded men during the last war lost their faith in a heavenly Father.

Yes, what kind of answer do we Christians have to this question? It seems as if all that remains is the difference between the Old Testament and the New Testament texts: that we cannot believe in an almighty Father but rather that God is either almighty or he is a kind Father. Either the Old Testament or the New Testament text must be right. Either God does not will all this dreadfulness which is now going on because he is a kind Father but a weak, powerless one who can do nothing; or God could stop it all if he wanted to do so but does not—then he is not a kind Father but a cruel tyrant of the world, insensible to human suffering, against whom one can do nothing, against whom one can only rear up in defiance. Or—and this is the conclusion that many draw— there is actually no god. Your faith in God, we hear everywhere, is refuted by world history. Your God is a phantasy, unreal. Your phantasy is, to be sure, more beautiful than reality—O were you right! Unfortunately it is not so but only a dream from which the harsh facts of reality again and again awaken us.

I believe, dear friends, there is no one at all among us who has not these days followed one or the other line of thought. It is therefore important that we honestly come to terms with this question and determine for what purpose our double text is necessary. We simply have to know how the almightiness and fatherly love of God are related. Do they belong together? Dare we confess, "I believe in God the Father Almighty"? Either we have an answer to this question or our faith will always be undecided in its content and uncertain in its foundation. "I am the Lord, and there is no other. I form light and create darkness, I make weal and create woe, I am the Lord, who do all these things." God is therefore almighty because he is the creator. Out of nothing God created the world. That is the message not only of the Old Testament but just as much so that of the New Testament. God would not really be God if there were something beside him that limited his will. Then he would not really be the only God. A God, however, who is not the only God is just an idol. Therefore, both—unseparated—belong in the text: "I am the Lord, and there is no other." The God who is creator, the Lord God, is the only God. There is no other. Of course the world is beside him; there is a nature that is not God; there are laws of nature that really rule the course of nature; there are creatures and among them are we men who are really not God but, so to speak, opposite God. But we are not a boundary for God's almightiness because he himself has created us. Because he has created us, he has in a certain sense limited his own almightiness. Because he has given us a free will, individual decision, even the ability to say no to him, he has, so to speak, laid out a free space for us just as a father makes room in his workshop for his children where they may work, learn to be independent and to accept responsibility for themselves. In this area they may now rule and manage. Their father does not always speak to them there, even when they make stupid mistakes or ruin a good piece of wood or dull many beautiful tools. How else would they ever grow up if they did not learn for themselves what are the consequences of mistakes?

So God deals with us. God lets us decide for ourselves, but he also lets us take the consequences of our decisions. "What man sows he must also reap." And that is what again and again frightens us, that there is so much suffering in the world. It frightens us and makes us doubt our faith because we do not want to see how much guilt, how much folly, how much disobedience against God's commandment, there is in the world. God does not create the disobedience, the folly, or the guilt, but he does create their consequences. He has so ordered the world and so controls it that suffering is the consequence of sin. If, however, God had allowed as much suffering as there ought to be as the consequence of our sin, we all long ago would have been cast into hell, which we all richly deserve. It is only because of God's patience and goodness that he allows us to go on living in order that we may change.

But why, then, does he spare one person more than another? Why is there so much suffering of innocent people? Why is suffering so unequally divided? Why do the godless often suffer the least and the godly the most? Why . . . Yes, let me go on, why does God not rule the world just as I think it should be? Why did God not ask me how to run the world so it would have turned out so much better, how to run things according to my superior intelligence? Do you not see what kind of advice we are giving God? As if God had to account to us, as if we were in a position to say how the world ought to be ruled so that it would turn out well with all! So this pride would be silenced once for all, God has placed the cross of the Savior before our eyes. See there how God works, how so completely incomprehensible in his wisdom, justice, and love. That was, to be sure, unjust suffering. It was—humanly speaking—nonsense, stupidity that happened there. And even *this,* God has made to be the relevation of his justice and love, as nothing else. What we see is this: God there punishes our sins and also reveals his forgiveness. There is nothing in the world that can more deeply convince us of our guilt and make us so sorry as the crucifixion of Jesus— just as nothing can so quiet a defiant child as when it sees its mother shed tears over it in trouble. The vicarious suffering of the mother cuts more deeply into its heart than its own suffering. And so nothing can press the love of God into our hearts as the death of the Savior because we see there what all God's love takes upon itself for us. Nothing can prove love so well for us as suffering willingly taken over for us. So the most senseless thing in itself—that we hanged the Holy God as a religious criminal, as a godless man, on a criminal's gallows—becomes a revelation of God's justice and love.

There we can, I say, see how incomprehensible God's rule of the world is, how he uses strange means that we would never have chosen, that we would never have thought of. From that, however, we must recognize how great is God's love and wisdom, that he has done it in that way and not as we would have done it. The cross of the Savior is the work of God. He has created this "evil," this "woe," as our text from Isaiah says. But that does not do away with the fact that it is at the same time the sinful work of men. The cross was the consequence of Judas' treason, of the jealousy and blindness of the high priests, of the human fears of the Roman governor. Yet it was God's work.

So also God creates in this time of struggle and misery. His work is everything that happens, as formerly he remained the Almighty, the Creator and Ruler of the world. In his hand are the mighty who still rule at present; in his hand are the godless, the cruel, the fierce, before whose increase we all shudder. They are all chessmen on his chessboard; they do not know it. They think they are playing their own game, and we also think so, of ourselves and of the other ones. And in a certain sense it is true that they are. We live by our own calculations. Nevertheless, God uses us all as the tools for his own plans, the good and the evil, the harmless and the great evildoers. How he does that is his secret. We could not understand it even if he explained it to us; he really would be explaining it to us as children. He explains only as much as we can understand: first, that suffering is the consequence of human sin and that it should warn us against evil so that we abandon it and return; secondly, that all the suffering and woe that he uses as a means to accomplish his purpose cannot abolish his plan which he has revealed to us in Jesus Christ as the plan of redemption.

For that is now the real revelation of God: "See what love the Father has given us, that we should be called the children of God; and so we are." The main point is not that God uses the treason of Judas, the false sentence of the high court, Pilate's fear of men, as true as that is also; rather, that God when he creates and uses all this evil also reveals his love and accomplishes his work of salvation. For that reason Jesus Christ came, "that he might destroy the works of the devil," that he might abolish the evil in which all of us are entangled and establish the eternal life, the Kingdom of God where there is no more suffering and even where death will no longer be. We cannot see ahead, and even then we shall understand only partly why God has taken this way toward his goal, why he allows wars and godless tyrannies. One day, when we open our eyes on the other side, we shall perhaps understand a little or at least as much as we creatures are capable of understanding or still have a need to understand. But this much is certain: God goes as he freely wills toward his goal. As a stream flowing toward the sea follows many crooked and unbelievably roundabout ways to get to its goal because the formation of the land does not allow a direct way, so God goes over the land of human history by a winding way toward his goal because the land formation of human sin, of human rebellion against God, does not allow a more direct way. But as sure as the stream flows seaward even when it seems to be flowing for long stretches away from the sea, equally certain is the way of God with humanity toward the Kingdom of God, toward eternity, toward the goal of perfect fellowship between him and the creature.

The almightiness of God and his love do not stand in opposition to one another but in a reciprocal relation. Were God not almighty, how could we trust that he could really carry out his plan of love? Were God not love, how could we ever call him God? After we have once seen Jesus Christ we can call no one else God except him who is love. It is of course true that the Old Testament emphasizes the almightiness of God and is not able to present the love of God with the same clarity as the New Testament. For God had still not given us the most extreme demonstration of his love. He had not yet come to us as man and had not yet as man taken upon himself our sins and guilt. That is what John means when he says: "See what love the Father has given us." Only on the basis of this gift do we know how limitless and unconditional is the love of God; only upon it can we say with complete trust in spite of our sinfulness: God is still my Father; I am still his child.

And what now is the practical consequence? The most important thing that can be said to us in this time and must be said is this: all that which the world shows you cannot separate you from him whom Jesus

Christ shows you. That we do not waver in this faith is now the most important thing of all. Were we to lose this faith, we would have lost everything. Then life would have no more meaning for us. Life has, however, exactly this meaning, that we live in this faith in the Father Almighty humbly and with love. Before the almightiness of God we become humble, for then we know how insignificant we are, how dependent we are upon God's acting and giving. Not upon ourselves, thank God, depends the salvation of the world; not in our hands is the destiny of the world. Not upon us does it depend what becomes of humanity. Completely beyond our understanding, God can carry out his plan through a Judas. We are not really those upon whom it depends. But we dare not therefore precipitate anything or become discouraged. For what God has planned we know through Jesus Christ. Just as he has redeemed us in him, so he will redeem the whole world in him. Even if we do not control the destiny of the world, we may still know that God has sent us his love and will do so more and more so we may be fellow workers in his works. We may proclaim his love to others; we may lead them to him. Even our love, though it is still so incomplete, points to his love. We may be joyful and certain not only in our faith in God's love but also in the fellowship that he has given us, that foretaste of what the end of all things will be. We may love those who doubt the love of God so that we may be a help to them in believing that love is still the only ultimate truth. The more we love, the less they can doubt God's love, the more they must ask about him who sends us such love in the midst of a loveless world. When we are steadfast in the love of God something new around us will take place in the world as a parable of what it will sometime be "when God is all in all." The one proof at present that God is the Father Almighty is a community of humble, loving children of God. And to be that is the meaning of this present life. Amen.

III The Light of the Nations

I believe . . . in Jesus Christ his only
Son our Lord.

It is too light a thing that you should be my servant to raise
up the tribes of Jacob and to restore the preserved of Israel;
I will give you as a light to the nations, that my salvation may
reach to the end of the earth. . . . I have kept you and given
you as a covenant to the people. (Isa. 49:6, 8.)

EVERY DAY WE think about the world of nations.
We have gradually learned that in sickness and prosperity we are united with one another in one body,
of which the words of the apostle are quite true: when
one member suffers all members suffer with him. We
Swiss know that our destiny is not dependent upon
us alone, nor solely upon the decisions of the nations
neighboring us. What is determined in the White

House in Washington, or in the Kremlin, can from one day to the next work itself out in every Swiss household and in the most remote village of the Confederation for good or evil. The time of national isolation is over forever; the nations, whether they like it or not, have become destiny's one sole community. That is one fact that no one can any longer alter. But what has this fact to do with God, with the message of Jesus Christ, with the Bible?

Our text gives us an answer to that question. Two and a half thousand years ago when the people of Israel were forcefully moved to Babylon after the destruction of Jerusalem by Nebuchadnezzar and there, far from home and far from the Temple, threatened to sink into hopelessness and discouragement, God gave them a prophet who dared to deliver the word of God about the coming salvation and to inspire his downcast people again with hope and courage from God. "Comfort, comfort my people"— so begins his writing, which is preserved for us in ch. 40 of The Book of Isaiah. This prophet whose name we do not even know, let alone the story of his life, was given by God as the first man upon the earth to speak of the nations and of the history of the nations as of one unity, something that formed a congruous whole. Considered from a purely human point of view, one has to count this man whom people call, at loss for a better name, the Second Isaiah, among the greatest discoverers, for he has discovered the fact of "world history." He himself, however, would protest against such a title of honor and say: I have discovered nothing at all. What I speak, God has commanded me to speak; not my discovery but his word I pass on. He who has created all the nations is also the Lord of them all. And he has created them all so that they may all know him as their Lord and live by his love. As they all have this one common origin, so they all have this one common goal. From this we know what the ancient Greeks did not know in spite of all their wisdom: that there is one connected humanity and one world history running toward *one* goal. That is why the Christian faith—and were it just the faith of the dearest little mother who reads the Bible and prays in her little bedroom—always has this great horizon including all nations and knows that the Kingdom God created is one body from many nations, and every one of us a member of it.

Thus the Lord speaks: It is too light a thing that you should be my servant to raise up the tribes of Jacob and to restore the preserved of Israel; I will give you as a light to the nations, that my salvation may reach to the end of the earth. That, dear friends, is the foundation charter of missions. Roughly in the year 550 before Jesus Christ that happened. Since then there have been missions to the heathen. Since then those who belong to the community of God have known that there is no private Christianity, and no mere national Christianity, but one church owing the gospel to all nations of the world.

About whom does this word of God really talk

when it speaks of and to the servant of God? Sometimes it seems as if the prophet of the Babylonian captivity means the people of Israel; they, the stricken, tormented people of God enduring alone by God's grace and holding together through the knowledge of God, shall be God's servant among the nations. But then again there are many other passages, as precisely our text is one, where quite clearly the distinction is made between God's people and the servant of God. One could think the prophet means himself; he is the one addressed by God as "my servant." But even this interpretation does not suffice. Rather, we must turn back to the old view of the first Christian community: the servant of God whom Deutero-Isaiah has seen five hundred and fifty years before Christ's birth is no other than Jesus Christ our Lord. And the book of this prophet is a genuine Advent book, and this prophet a genuine Advent man. He sees, we cannot comprehend at all how that is possible, things that are not yet, that will only happen in the distant future, five hundred and fifty years later— as if one saw in the year 1400 what is now happening in the year 1959. From such a distance in the past he sees the picture of a servant, of a servant of God, of a suffering one, of a man who is laden with the guilt of humanity in order to bear it for man. And now he says of this servant: he is the light of the nations; he is the salvation of the world! It is something quite inconceivably great that in this dark past, in the midst of the time of despair of the people of Israel, this man may see over a half thousand years away to proclaim the light of the nations and the salvation of the world. When we have once seen that, we notice that it is more or less so with the entire Old Testament. The entire Old Testament is an Advent book. It deals with the coming of God, with the coming of his Kingdom; still veiled, only in silhouettes of the coming One, it proclaims the Messiah, the message of God who comes to his people, to the nations in order to be with them.

Why has God done it thus, dear friends? Why has he first sent the Old and then the New Testament, why first the prophets and then Jesus Christ, why first the imperfect and then the perfect? The Bible itself gives us an answer to this question. That is so because we are a headstrong, hard-of-hearing, hard-to-handle people. God has to have an infinite amount of patience with us. He has to begin right at the beginning, and only gradually can he give us the full light. We would not have been able to understand his word at all without the long time of preparation in the old covenant. And a second thing: it indicates in this how God has the whole history of the world in his hand, how he allows his light to rise slowly out of the dark, as he wills. That is a real comfort to us in the present time. Does it not happen sometimes that you think: What kind of patience the Lord God must have with us that he has not yet rejected me and that he does not say, "Now it's the end; now I have had enough of you!" And he has patience; that is why he has not already allowed the end of the world to come, as the apostles expected it. He has had two thousand years of patience until now so that we can mend our ways, so that we repent. So forbearing and patient is the Lord! But do you not notice that God's forbearance should lead you to repentance?

Even the prophet of the exile did not think that it would still take six hundred years until *He* came whom he foresaw as God's servant. The true prophets are not soothsayers, and true Biblical prophecy is not a calculation of the future; and that is why they who thought they could calculate future events from Biblical prophecies have always been disappointed. This apocalyptic long division has nothing to do with Biblical faith. For day and hour—even year and century— no one knows, not even the Son; the Father alone knows, says the Lord Jesus. But if the prophet did not know even the year, not even the century, then he did know very well the work and the meaning of the coming Messiah. "I will give you as a light to the nations. . . . I have . . . given you as a covenant to the people." Jesus Christ is the revealer of the divine truth and he is the redeemer from guilt and sin.

During wartime blackout practices we noticed what life would be like without light, how weird everything was, how one took uncertain steps, how quickly one lost his way, how easily one collided. The blackout is said to have cost more lives in England than the war. That may be a parable for us of what darkness in the spiritual sense means in the individual life of man and in the life of nations. You know, indeed, how it is when it is simply dark in us and around us, when we do not know in and out, when it is like a devilish darkening over our mind, and we ourselves think, feel, and do what the light shuns. That the Bible calls "wandering in darkness." But it can happen that one becomes accustomed to this darkness so that he does not notice how terrible, how inhuman, how contrary to sense all life then becomes. And as in individuals, so in the life of nations. Now is a blackout time in the whole world of nations, as perhaps never at all before. For earlier one still knew that there is a God, that there is a righteousness, that finally a retribution comes, that there are holy laws and orders. But today there are millions and millions of Europeans— about the others I do not wish to speak now—who no longer know all that, who have radically struck God from their hearts and lives and who therefore live entirely in darkness and who do the works of darkness. We see today—and thank God; many who did not see it are now finally beginning to see it—that one cannot live without God. But perhaps it is already too late; perhaps the darkness of godlessness must first give vent to its fury before better times can come. The power of darkness seems today to have received a free night from God that it may crush to pieces what it wills so that the nations realize to what place one comes when he abolishes God. Perhaps even the Swiss nation must go through dreadful times of judgment so that it may also know how much it has wandered in the darkness, in its politics, in its business life, in its earning and distribution of money, in its amusements. Yes, who dares to affirm that we are not also the people "who sit in darkness"?

This darkness is all the worse, since we indeed have seen the light. Jesus Christ has indeed come; the world has received the message about him, has heard the announcement of the seeking, forgiving, redeeming love of God, has outwardly become a Christian world. What kind of guilt is it that things could go so far in Christian Europe as they have now gone? If we could seek information from God who is to be made responsible in the first place, do you believe he would name Lenin, Stalin, Hitler? I fear very much he would say: "You Christians are guilty! If you had been genuine Christians, then there need never have been a Bolshevism or a National Socialism." If we Christians had more Christian communism, as the time of the apostles shows it to us, communistic sharing—"What is mine is yours; you are my brother!"— then we should not now have godless communism, and if Christendom had created more of a community of nations, then we would not now need a community by force. If Christendom had really subjected itself to the dictatorship of the Holy Spirit, then there would now be no dictatorship by brutal men. If Christendom had really been Christian, then there would now be no movement of the godless. So God's opinion of us may run.

Is that all that God would give us for an answer? God never judges and punishes merely to judge and to punish. He does it in order to call us to repentance; he does it so that we finally begin to take him seriously. How can we take God seriously otherwise than when we truly accept *him* whom he has sent us as Light and Mediator of the covenant? The light that God has sent the nations in Jesus Christ has not gone out; the new covenant, the covenant of reconciliation, of redemption, of peace that he has made in him the Mediator of the covenant with the human race, continues. It matters only that we see the light and that we really allow ourselves to be taken up in the covenant and remain loyal to it. Jesus Christ is given to us for righteousness, for sanctification, and for redemption, and it is just as true today as two thousand years ago: if one is in Christ, then he is a new creature. But it must also become true among us; we must really wrap ourselves up in the grace of God in Jesus Christ just as a little child, when it becomes afraid, wraps itself up in the apron of its mother, has a good cry there, and is also comforted so that it again jumps happily into the street.

The other day there came to me a man who had suffered many years terribly under the power of darkness. But this time he looked at me as I have never seen him and said: "It is gone." I said: "What is gone?" Then he told me how he grasped for the Bible in his despair, read well a dozen times one after another the letter to the Romans. All at once it became bright in him. The power of darkness had gone away; he understood that it was true for him what Jesus

The Light of the Nations 47

Christ says on the cross: "It is finished." "Since I have understood that," he said to me, "all is gone, the old tie, sin, anxiety. I am a happy, free man!" See, he has wrapped himself up in Jesus Christ and has thereby become a new man. There are, in fact, men here who can testify the same of themselves. Such a thing happens to us when we really place, plunge our heart, our thinking, our feeling, our willing, our imagination in Jesus Christ. As different men, as new men, we go forth from this encounter with him. He is still really the light and the salvation of the world. It is still true today: "He who follows me will not walk in darkness, but will have the light of life." We are in darkness in so far as we are away from Christ, and in the light in so far as we live in Christ.

But now it is the nature of light that it extends itself. He who lives with Jesus Christ not only *has* light but also becomes a light—and were it only a modest little candlelight for others. This light is given to us not only for ourselves but for all nations. As light of the nations he has come that his salvation may reach to the ends of the earth. The Christian community must always prove that it really has the light by carrying it farther to the ends of the earth. From the very beginning the Christian community was a missionary society. It could not keep for itself what was given to it; it had to pass it on. For just as the power of darkness shuts one off, so the strength of the light of Christ opens one up for others. Light shines, light spreads. Thus the light of Jerusalem encroached upon all Palestine, then upon the Near East; it spread to Greece, to Rome, to Spain, to Africa. Thus it also came to us in Switzerland. And thus it also goes to-day from Switzerland and other lands out into all parts of the world. Missionary zeal was always a ther-mometer for the warmth of the Christian faith. When missionary zeal becomes lame, then faith has also be-come lame and love cooled down.

In the present time, however, we have a double cause to carry on the work of missions with all zeal. We see what godlessness causes in the world of na-tions. For the sake of ourselves we have to carry on the mission to all nations; for what shall become of Europe if the already existing powers of godlessness also join with the nations of the East that more or less help determine the destiny of the nations upon the whole earth? Out of prudence we may wish that China, Japan, and India will be penetrated as soon as possible by the spirit of the gospel. But as a Chris-tian community we cannot and must not take refuge in such a thought. Already the thought lies closer to us that perhaps in those distant nations the treasure of the gospel will be preserved more safely than in Europe threatened by Bolshevism. In times of up-heaval one hides the costliest treasures in the safest places. It already seems as if the Far East would be a safer place for the message of Christ than our Europe decaying so much into godlessness. But even that can-not be our last thought. We owe quite simply the message of salvation to all nations. We sin against them and the gospel if we do not bring it to them. We have no right to keep it to ourselves. Never can the community of Christ fall into the thought: We now have so much to do in our own land and need so much money that there is no longer anything for the missions. Before God, Switzerland is no more important than China or India. For the church there are no national barriers and no national partialities. The mission is not the concern of some who have a particular interest for such a thing; rather, it is the concern of the whole community of Christians wherever it is and of every member of the community of Christians, whoever he is. No one has a right to exclude himself. Either you are willing to have missions or you are no Christian. That his salvation may go to the ends of the earth, for that, dear friends, every one of us is together responsible. Awake, thou Spirit of the first witnesses! Amen.

IV God
Became Man

Who was conceived by the Holy Ghost,
born of the Virgin Mary.

*When the time had fully come, God sent forth his Son, born
of woman, born under the law, . . . so that we might receive
adoption as sons. And because you are sons, God has sent
the Spirit of his Son into our hearts, crying, "Abba! Father!"
So through God you are no longer a slave but a son, and if a
son then an heir. (Gal. 4:4-7.)*

IF WE TODAY in the midst of a time of world
struggle wish to celebrate Christmas properly, then
two things dare not happen. First, we dare not let the
joy of Christmas be corrupted by thoughts about the
horrors of the present time and by anxiety about the
still greater ones that may yet come. Then the devil
would have gained what he wants. With a Chris-

tianity that has no more joy in its heart he has an easy game. The only thing that he really fears are men who carry the real joy of Christmas in their hearts. For against them he is powerless. All evil thrives only in joylessness. When the evil enemy attacks a man who can truly sing out from his heart:

> The Sun that laughs at me
> Is my Lord Jesus Christ;
> What makes me sing
> Is what is in heaven,

then that enemy stands before a fortress against which all his weapons can do nothing. He has to surrender in despair. That is why his tactic always is that he first tries to rob us of this joy. The second thing, however, is just as important: that we are not sucked into an artificial Christmas joy, that so-called Christmas joy which is gone two days after Christmas, which lasts about as long as the candles we burn on the Christmas tree. "One must now forget what kind of evil time it is; it should at least be Christmas today." This Christmas joy belongs in the category "means of intoxication, narcotic." It produces only illusion and disappointment, and leaves the soul empty and weak. Against it the old evil enemy has nothing at all to protest. On the contrary, to him it is all right, for he loves everything that is illusion; all that plays into his hand.

No, dear friends, we wish to have, if I may so express it, a solid Christmas joy, not just a little candle-light with a Christmas-tree fragrance, but a storm lan-

tern that does not go out even when it is blown upon
from all sides. And that is why I have chosen for today a text that has nothing at all to do with the poetry
of Christmas but is one of the most powerful words
of the entire Holy Scriptures because it, as it were,
expresses the Christmas joy in the whole context of
the message of salvation. That I would like to try to
show you with God's help. May he who gave this word
to the apostle also make it so sink into our hearts that
it will stand fast, invincible, not to be brought down,
a truly mighty fortress that is able to ward off all
attacks.

"When the time had fully come . . ." How remarkable that still sounds! Time that had fully come!
How altogether differently we speak of time! Every
man speaks today of an evil time. One would like to
be away from it, either back in a more beautiful past
or far away in a happier future. It is only the time that
is now which one does not like to live through. That
is quite humanly understandable, just as a sick person
yearns for days when he was well or when he will
again be well. This is now the time of humanity's
sickness: the body is running a fever and is in pain;
it tosses and turns in the dreadful events of the present. But how did we do before with time? Was the
time before a time that had fully come? Why, then,
these efforts to pass away the time, to forget the lost
time, the elapsed time? Why was it and why is it still
that so many men complain they have no time? Think
once a little about what a role the "too late" or "too

early" has played in your life, or about why it is that the memory of the past is so sad. Time passes and with it our expectations and hopes, unfulfilled, just as buds fall from the trees without having become fruit. Just that seems to be the nature of time, which we all know: that it has not fully come but—just passes away. And now there it sounds like a tone from another world into our world: "When the time had fully come . . . "

Yes, from another world, and yet it means that from our world and from our world time. It was not at all a particularly good time about which the apostle speaks. Had one then said to some Jew, "You, the time has now fully come," he would have looked at him as one looks at a crazy man. What has fully come? Nothing has fully come. The world is full of suffering, anxiety, injustice, death, and sorrow. Because in an obscure corner of the Roman Empire a little child has come into the world—therefore has the time fully come? Are we Jews not the prey of Roman imperialism? Do the nations not groan under the yoke of Roman dictatorship? Do the Roman officials not plunder our land? And if we were to meet this Jew again thirty years later, would he not scornfully call to us: "And now where are you with your time that has fully come? Yesterday he was crucified by the Roman governor, your fulfiller of time, and now things go on the same old miserable way." And since then nineteen hundred years has flown by, with numerous wars; the world empire of Rome has broken up; others have come and gone. Millions of men have been born and have died. What do you want with your absurd "when the time had fully come"? Time passes away—that is all.

And yet it is true: when the time had fully come, God sent his Son. We cannot see that the time had fully come. But above time God sits on his throne in his eternity and looks upon the world and its time, just as a doctor sits at the bed of a sick person who lies there in fever and knows nothing of the doctor. But the doctor listens carefully to his breathing and takes his pulse and then at a particular moment stands up and calls his nurse and says, "Now is the time; now we shall operate." And then he performs the saving act. We do not know the time when it is time for God; we are the sick person, not the physician. But God knows the time, our time, which is his time. Time for him to act, to save. When the time had fully come, God sent his Son.

That is why we celebrate Christmas. For we know: at that time the saving act took place. Just why at that time, we do not really understand. But we know what God has done at that time for us, a humanity sick unto death. He has saved us. And the act by which he has done it is the coming of him whom the Bible calls the Son of God. That is, as everything that we say about God, a parable. God has no sons just as men have sons. But this parable expresses a truth that we can never completely grasp. It says: Jesus is he who comes forth from the heart and mystery of God, yes, who is God himself upon earth, without God having ceased to be in his eternity; he, in whom God himself is with us and wills to be with us, and in whom he himself speaks to us and deals with us; he in whom God himself encounters us and opens his heart, he through whom God has established the relation with himself.

As a true man, he was among us, one of us. That Paul wants to say with the words "born of woman, born under the law." Both are expressions that designate man as a creature, as an ordinary man. That is what can be said of every man and must be said: he is born of woman and born under the law. The apostle does not speak of a virgin either here or anywhere else. He does not want to emphasize what distinguishes Jesus from us, but rather, what makes him like us: birth and law. He was once a little struggling child in swaddling clothes. And he had to learn, had to listen, had to go to school to learn to read and write; had to learn, as every other little Jewish boy, to read the Bible—the Old Testament. He was reared in the custom and religion of his father, perhaps also in his father's vocation as a carpenter. His mother taught him to pray, and he prayed his whole life long. His last word, "My God, my God, why hast thou forsaken me?" was a prayer. He died, as every man must die, and was buried. He was a man. Thus God wanted to have it; as man, God wanted to come to us men; otherwise he would not really come to us at all. Only a man can we really understand. We do not under-

stand what is less than a man, and we do not understand what is more than a man. But God wanted to
be wholly understandable to us, and near. Thus he
came as man to us.

But now this "under the law" has still another far-
reaching meaning. By law Paul means in Galatians the
curse that weighs upon human life on account of its
godlessness. Into this curse Jesus came, just as a son
comes into the business debts of his father. He himself
did not indeed incur the debts, but the debts that
men have incurred crush him to death. He came into
it, and the curse that lies upon the whole human race
on account of its godlessness destroys him. For that
reason he had come. He, the innocent one, wanted
and had to be destroyed by an evil human inheritance.

See, that belongs to the message of Christmas!
There is no Christmas without Good Friday; we will
also see that there is no Good Friday without Easter
and Whitsunday. That is the most powerful thing
about this Christmas text, that it unites Christmas
with Good Friday, Easter, and Whitsundy. The incarnation of the Savior is first completed on the cross.
For there for the first time it is completely true: he
took us upon himself in order to give himself.

Here the apostle speaks of a kind of slave transac-
tion, as if one goes to the slave market, stands before
a slave and says to the slavetrader, "Let him go free;
I will be the slave in his place;" and then he frees the
slave and takes the other who has voluntarily given
himself. So Jesus has come under the curse for us, has

borne it for us so that we may become free. That is the real incarnation. On Good Friday it has come about for the first time. So he has become one of our kind, one burdened with slavery, so that we may become those of his kind, free men, God's sons. This difficult basis our Christmas joy has. All the suffering and evil of time is, so to speak, crammed into it. That is why it is no cheap but a very expensive joy. It cost God his Son. God could not make it cheaper. This act was necessary if we should be saved. But the cost of his act he alone has borne.

Again and again we ask, Why? This question one can never finish answering. Yet the answer must be again and again this: Because God could not release us from the curse of sin any other way. Sin is basically only one thing: that we love ourselves instead of loving God and our neighbor. We are so entangled in this self-love that all education, all culture, all morality, and all training cannot release us from it. They become again for us all the means of self-love. God has seen—to say it like a child—that there is only one means to overcome this dreadful self-love of men: his love, which goes so far that he surrenders and sacrifices himself for us. Only this sacrifice is a great enough counterweight to the dreadful weight of our self-love. Only with this sacrifice could he break the curse that lies over us through godlessness. Thus he came to us as man; thus he completely entered into the curse of godlessness and allowed himself to be swallowed up by it—so that we may finally become free of it. How, then, does that happen? By finally venturing through this deed of divine self-sacrifice to believe in God's love so that we see the greatness of our guilt and yet at the same time no longer despair over it. For without Jesus Christ we do one of two things: either we believe in God's love as something self-evident, without seeing our guilt and repenting of our sin; or we see the guilt of our sin and with nothing but a feeling of guilt do not come to believe in God's love. Both things allow us to remain fixed in our godlessness. Only if we get away from both, from the false carelessness that regards God's love as self-evident and from the melancholy anxiety that despairs of God's love, only then are we free from the curse of sin. That cannot happen otherwise than through the knowledge of what God has done for us in Jesus Christ.

That is the purpose of the whole incarnation of God's Son, this exchange, that we gave him our curse and he gives us his divine Sonship. Through this redemption which has cost him his life we receive the freedom of God's sons. That is the title of nobility that we receive as a gift. Christ is by nature God's Son, not one who has become but one who is from all eternity. But we are adopted sons, we become sons through this bond, through this act of exchange. But we become sons only through the fact that we on our side sign this bill of sale, just as one completes the sale of a house before a notary public. Through it we say: "I acknowledge it in unspeakable thankfulness and at the same time in shame and repentance that out of a slave of godlessness, of self-love and of anxiety, I have become through you, Lord Jesus, a free man, a son of God, that which you are from eternity. Your love now belongs to me and your eternal life now belongs to me. No one may dispute that it belongs to me because you have bought it for me through your suffering of death."

See, that is the Christmas joy that has foundation! For where there is such faith, there Christmas and Good Friday are accompanied by Easter and Whitsunday. For not to the one who has died for me on the cross can I speak thus, but only to the one who has been raised from the grave, who sits at the right hand of God. If Jesus has not been raised, then indeed the trade is worth nothing, then indeed it was not God's Son but a mere man who could do nothing for me. But if he is God's Son, then he has also been raised and offers me his eternal life in exchange for the curse under which I live and for the death before which I tremble. But if I can really hear his voice so that the voice of my heart answers him, then to Easter is added Whitsunday, the festival of the Holy Spirit. For he does not speak to me down from heaven but to my heart, here and now; truly indeed in my heart he speaks. He says to me that I am his in eternity, and I on my side may answer with Christmas joy: "Praised be Jesus Christ who is my redeemer." To be God's sons, dear friends, if that is true, then we have a fortress in this world that no devil can overrun. Why, then, do we Christians sneak so morosely through the world? Why does it no longer radiate from our faces? Why is there so little warmth among us? Why otherwise than because we again and again forget it, again and again do not rightly believe that it is really and literally true: Abba, Father, "no longer a slave but a son, and if a son then an heir." But if we really believe it, and it becomes as true in our hearts as in that of the apostle because it is indeed the same Holy Spirit who says it to him and who says it to us, then we also may know something of the time that had fully come. When this love of God shines in this time which passes away, this evil time, then something of evil times and of the passing away of time disappears, then something flashes up from the other world that can never again be extinguished. And thereupon we then wish to celebrate Christmas in spite of the devil and evil times, and to our God sing songs of praise and thank him that he is so incomprehensibly merciful that he redeems us who have been subject to the law with the life of his own Son so that we may live with him as his free sons in eternity.   Amen.

V Suffered Under Pontius Pilate

[He] suffered under Pontius Pilate.

Then Pilate took Jesus and scourged him. And the soldiers plaited a crown of thorns, and put it on his head, and arrayed him in a purple robe; they came up to him, saying, "Hail, King of the Jews!" and struck him with their hands. Pilate went out again, and said to them, "Behold, I am bringing him out to you, that you may know that I find no crime in him." So Jesus came out, wearing the crown of thorns and the purple robe. Pilate said to them, "Here is the man!" When the chief priests and the officers saw him, they cried out, "Crucify him, crucify him!" Pilate said to them, "Take him yourselves and crucify him, for I find no crime in him." The Jews answered him, "We have a law, and by that law he ought to die, because he has made himself the Son of God." When Pilate heard these words, he was the more afraid; he entered the praetorium again and said to Jesus, "Where are you from?" But Jesus gave no answer. Pilate therefore said to him, "You will not

*speak to me? Do you not know that I have power to release
you, and power to crucify you?" Jesus answered him, "You
would have no power over me unless it had been given you
from above; therefore he who delivered me to you has the
greater sin."*

*Upon this Pilate sought to release him, but the Jews cried
out, "If you release this man, you are not Caesar's friend;
every one who makes himself a king sets himself against
Caesar." When Pilate heard these words, he brought Jesus
out and sat down on the judgment seat at a place called The
Pavement, and in Hebrew, Gabbatha. Now it was the day of
Preparation for the Passover; it was about the sixth hour. He
said to the Jews, "Here is your King!" They cried out, "Away
with him, away with him, crucify him!" Pilate said to them,
"Shall I crucify your King?" The chief priests answered, "We
have no king but Caesar." Then he handed him over to them
to be crucified. (John 19:1-16.)*

FIRST OF ALL it is a very strange fact that in the
Confession of Faith of the Christian church the name
of a Roman state official comes to the front. For what
has the Roman Empire to do with the Kingdom of
Heaven, a name that belongs only to world history
with the faith in him whose name is above every name
and in whom the eternal life is contained? Has the
church done the right thing when from the very beginning it has included the name of Pontius Pilate,
the imperial governor of Judea, in the short summary
of its gospel proclamation, which we call the Apostles'
Creed and which it has every Christian child mem-
orize so that the main thing may always be present in
his mind? We wish to let the answer to this question

be given to us by our text. In a time when the power conflicts of the kingdoms of this world make us hold our breath, when our daily life, private and public, is encroached upon and determined to such an enormous degree by the interests and demands of the state order, it is quite justifiable to reflect on how our Lord Jesus has met the state and the state the Lord Jesus. It is, indeed, something that makes us ponder that of all the Gospels, John's Gospel, which Luther calls the only really chief Gospel, tells about this meeting between the Savior and the imperial governor with much greater detail than everything else. Obviously the Evangelist sees in it something that is of the greatest importance to every believer.

In the chapter preceding our text a longer conversation between Pilate and the Lord Jesus is reported. His Jewish enemies had brought him after the short trial before the high priest and high court to the imperial Roman ruler so that he who alone had the law of the death penalty in his hands might ratify their sentence of death. Their charge is, of course, not clear but ambiguous: he passes himself off as the Messiah. That could mean he is making himself the king or he claims to be God's Son. Obviously the first track will be pursued at the start, for it should make the greatest impression on the statesman who has to protect the law of the emperor. That is the reason for the question of Pilate, "Are you the king of the Jews?" When he receives no clear answer to this inquiry, he changes the question: "So you are a king?" To this the

Lord now answers with a clear, "Yes, you say that I am a king." But what kind of king? The Roman jurist and statesman cannot help noticing that the issue here is not the state's legality and competence. "My kingship is not of this world"—was the answer to his first question. And the basis of the claim to be king runs: "For this I was born, and for this I have come into the world, to bear witness to the truth. Every one who is of the truth hears my voice." Now the statesman knows enough. Here he does not have to do with one who is grasping for the emperor's crown but with one who is grasping for his heart and his conscience. He forgets for a moment his imperial office and becomes a private citizen, a human being, however a human being who shuns this grasp from a world where he is powerless. He remembers suddenly his philosophical training which protects him from this personal grasp. With a half-scoffing, half-despairing confession of his philosophy which places all truth in question by the counterquestion, What is truth? he terminates the first conversation which became so weird for him. But he knows what he has to answer the Jews as an imperial advocate. "I find no crime in him." Release him! The imperial tribunal can do nothing else than acquit this Jesus.

But now the statesman has to experience that there is still another power—besides the imperial and besides that supraworld power that has met him in Jesus—the power of religious fanaticism. It roars: "Crucify him!" This power of religious passion is also a political danger. With it he has to reckon as a statesman. To the raging crowd he must throw a victim in order to appease it. He lets Jesus be scourged; he hands Him over to his soldiery that it may, so to speak, let its wantonness out on him for the diversion and appeasement of the fanaticism of the Jewish religion. The soldiers, always disposed to pranks, translate the court controversy into the grotesque. They force him, the accused Messiah, to wear a crown of thorns on his head, put on him a purple robe, and tender him scornful bows between ill-treatment.

Pilate hopes with that to have done enough for the Jews. Perhaps as a clever man of the world he thinks that the ridiculous may cool off the most intense passion. So he leads before the people the one made ridiculous by a crown of thorns, a purple robe, and bloody stripes in his face. "Behold the man!" And as the waves of wild passion again immediately strike against him—"Crucify, crucify!"—Pilate repeats once more what he has to say about the matter as an imperial judge: "I find no crime in him." He wishes to have nothing more to do with him—"Do with him what you will!"

But once again he encounters a new element that has come into play. "We have a law, and by that law he ought to die, because he has made himself the Son of God." If he was previously confronted simply by religious passion, then now it is the religious system, the religion of law, theological-juristic orthodoxy. In the system the living, present Son of God does not fit.

The system of religion of the Jews, secure in itself and making pious men secure, demands the removal of him who stands in the midst of them with the claim of divine power. One wants to have a God, but not one who comes too close. One wants to have a God with whom one can negotiate, a religion that consists of accomplishment and return, but not a God who breaks into our life as the living Lord and seizes upon something. Such a claim disturbs the balance of power; one must remove him. It can and dare not be that one is present who calls himself the Son of God.

"When Pilate heard these words, he was the more afraid." Obviously he feels again, but this time still more weirdly, that grasp for his heart and conscience from the other world that he does not know. Should there really be that, a man who dares to call himself the Son of God? Is God a reality so near and personal? That is why he asks Jesus, "Where are you from?" He receives no answer. And when he now threateningly calls attention to his power to release Jesus or to hand him over to death on the cross, Pilate receives an answer which he would have last expected: "You would have no power over me unless it had been given you from above; therefore he who delivered me to you has the greater sin." "Upon this"—so it continues—"Pilate sought to release him."

With that we have reached the high point of the story, so far as it touches on the encounter between the Roman governor and the Lord Jesus. We want to pause and ask ourselves, What has really happened

here? The last words of the Lord, which obviously
made the deepest impression of all on Pilate, show
us that here two realms completely foreign to each
other do not simply conflict with each other—the
Kingdom of God and the kingdom of the world—
rather, that between both, different as they are, there
is an inner bond. For the imperial Roman procura-
tor appears here suddenly in a completely new light,
no longer only as an opponent of Jesus in the battle
between God's Kingdom and the world, no longer
only as a neutral spectator who seeks to avoid the
question of truth, and no longer only as the private
individual disquieted by this weird truth, but as an
instrument of the divine will. The power to condemn and crucify Jesus Christ has been conferred
upon Pilate, upon the Roman State, by God. The
Roman State is an instrument of God; what this Roman state official does he does without knowing it is
the commission of God. How shall we understand
that?

First, we could think of what the apostle Paul has
written later in the thirteenth chapter of the letter
to the Romans, that all authority, all state power, is
from God, namely, from God for the administration
of the order of law that forces us to obey. We live in
a hard, evil, sinful world, and the evil that lives in all
men is of the kind that wholly annihilates us, so that
we would mutually destroy ourselves in a struggle
for existence if a power were not there that at least
forces men into an external order and justice. Were

only the divine love effective in us, were there only
good will among us, then we would need no state order of law to force us. The force of law is necessary
because of our sinfulness. And now I ask you not to
think: Certainly there are such criminal natures, such
insubordinate subjects who do the right thing only
when forced. Just think how difficult it is for us to
make the sacrifices that are necessary for a just distribution of the burdens of life in our nation. If the
state would not compel the payment of taxes, then
there would now be a very bad situation with regard
to our responsibility for the poor, for the unemployed,
for the public school. Yes, we Christians have accustomed ourselves to wait until the state forces us to do
what should be done. And how often has the Christian
community shown the world the shameful spectacle
of offering resistance to certain laws of social com-
pensation quite simply because they dug into its own
purse. By itself the purse did not want to open; it had
to be opened by the state. If we are not voluntarily
ready to pay for great sacrifices in the presence of the
underprivileged, then we shall live to see, perhaps
through revolution, a state constitution by which we
are not left with much of what we now call our prop-
erty. Revolutions always come from the same source
as the power of the state itself, namely, from the unwillingness to make voluntary sacrifices. The state is
therefore the compulsory equalizer used in God's
providence that establishes a raw, but nevertheless a
certain, justice. Let us think when the large unwel-

comed pages of the tax declaration come flying once
again into our house that they are really a repentance
sermon. "So hardhearted are you that you need the
compulsory justice of the state because your voluntary justice is so little." That is why the apostle Paul
admonishes his Roman congregation to pay the taxes
voluntarily and not merely from fear of punishment
to be expected otherwise. For behind the tax collector
may stand the will of God.

The state with all its cold justice, with its force, its
power and its compulsion, a servant of God! And indeed, the pagan Roman State, which does not know
the God who so uses it as his instrument, the Roman
governor Pilate who does not know God and does not
want to know him. To him God has given the power
that he has. But with that we have not yet arrived at
the real mystery of our text. Although the apostle
thinks solely of the state's legal order in that thirteenth chapter of Romans, which, as he says, punishes
the evil and rewards the good, our text speaks indeed
of the authority given by God to Pilate to crucify
Jesus Christ, God's Son. Here is meant not the just
state but the obviously unjust one. For in so far as
Pilate judges the case as a Roman jurist and statesman, Jesus receives, indeed, a clear acquittal. Before
the state's law Jesus is not guilty.

Even that belongs to the mysterious powers of divine providence, that the state had to declare before
all the world the innocence of Jesus. From the mouth
of the Roman State's head himself the world has heard

this acquittal. He is not guilty. On the contrary, it becomes quite clear from the last words of Jesus to his judge that before the divine tribunal Pilate stands as the accused. Jesus tells him to his face that he has sinned when he judged him, even if it is a smaller sin than that of those who have compelled this blood sentence from him. The roles of the accuser and the accused are therefore exchanged. From the examining judge, Pilate has suddenly become the condemned. The signature of Pilate under the high-priestly blood sentence is a judicial murder, and indeed essentially a premeditated one. Pilate knows quite well that he is acting against the law, that objective justice is not guiding him but anxiety about eventually unpleasant consequences that an acquittal of Jesus could have for him in Rome. He stands, therefore, at last as a weakling and judicial murderer, even though extenuating circumstances are intentionally made prominent by Jesus himself.

But in spite of the fact that it is an unjust sentence that is spoken out of human fear and not out of judicial consciousness, the Lord says here: "In allowing me to be put on the cross—by a wholly unjust way— you are acting without knowing it in the divine commission. You are carrying out God's plan. The sentence 'guilty of death,' which you are at last signing, is also signed by God. God is leading you with his pen." God wants to have it thus. His Son shall be hung as a criminal, not only by the representatives of religion but also by the representative of the state.

God himself strikes his Son on the cross through the hand of Pilate.

Is that not a horrible thought? Yes, dear friends, actually horrible until we comprehend what God wants to tell us. All that from the arrest in the Garden of Gethsemane on, the spitting and ill-treatment of the high council, the crown of thorns, the scourging, the mocking, finally the tortures of the crucifixion and the abandonment by all, at last by God himself —all that "Christ had to suffer." God wanted it so, God did that, and all the persons on the stage of this story of suffering—Judas, Caiaphas, the roaring crowd of people, the soldiers, and Pilate—they are all only instruments in God's hand who do what God wants to have done and what God wants to have done for our sakes. You can understand it only in the moment when you add to everything—"for me." Only then does it cease to be horrible, only then do you notice that you are horrible; but God who does all this is the Love that seeks and saves you.

Let us, however, turn back once more to Pilate. It is not just an accident that Pilate stands in the Apostles' Creed. With that a twofold thing is said: First, here the history of the world becomes the history of God's Kingdom, and the history of God's Kingdom, the history of the world. Here the Lord of all history invades with his holy history into profane history. The representative of the greatest world kingdom that has ever existed becomes here an instrument in the history of redemption. So real is the salvation of God and so superior love over the curse. That is the one thing. Secondly, Jesus Christ was not permitted to perish in a horrible way by choice. He had to be sentenced by a court. It was allowed to execute a death sentence on him. Why? Because you should be judged. This death sentence is intended for you, for you are deserving of death before God. You are a judged and condemned person. But now God loves you as you cannot comprehend. And to save you from the evil that must necessarily and rightly come upon you, he has surrendered his Son to this evil. This death is a punishment—not for him but for you. But this punishment he takes for you so that you may go unpunished and receive God's love and eternal life if you do only one thing—say yes to this punishment and give thanks from your heart for this love of God that does this for you.

Let us in conclusion, however, meditate on those other little words of the creed: *suffered* under Pontius Pilate. We see the picture of this suffering before us. Why, then, did this have to be? Why in addition to death torture, and in addition to torture scorn? Of course even here we can only repeat the first answer: "All that for your sake." But in the New Testament we always encounter wherever it speaks about the suffering of Christ still one other thought. The Lord has gone this way before us so that we may walk joyfully behind him when we are faring badly; so that we then know: now I too may go a little of the way the Lord Jesus has gone for me.

It will indeed be the case that the more one walks behind Jesus Christ as one for whom he has broken a pathway into new life, into God's love, the more one will also find it difficult. Life with Christ and for Christ is no promenade from joy to joy. Rather, it means: "He who wants to be my disciple must take up his cross." One cannot be a disciple without being one who bears a cross. That means first of all that the trouble that befalls us, as it does other people, we bear in a different spirit, namely, with secret joy—beneath tears—that we indeed walk behind our Lord Jesus Christ along his way. But then it also means that he who really is a disciple receives special difficulties and sufferings that follow by necessity from his being a disciple, so that these sufferings are therefore the stamp of his discipleship.

Not every suffering is that cross which the disciples must bear, of which he says, "Take it upon yourselves," but only the sufferings by which it becomes recognizable that we are disciples—persecution on account of our faith, mockery, estrangement from earlier friends, branding as a hypocrite and sneak. Just as one recognizes a peasant by his rough hands and his sunburned face, so one should recognize us Christians by the fact that we suffer for our Lord Christ. But is it not true that of this there is very little to be seen among us? Why? Quite simply because we still take much too lightly our service to Christ. If a farmer stays at home, then he can keep his hands fine and his skin white; if we Christians make it comfortable for ourselves to be Christians, hesitate and are afraid to bear witness to our Lord, squeeze around drawing the conclusions of our Christian faith, then we can escape suffering. But only so. By that every one of us may prove how faithfully he walks or does not walk behind his Lord.

Thus to us the crown of thorns the soldiers of Pilate placed on the Lord is not only the great comfort of Jesus, "All that I have done for you," but also his earnest exhortation, "What will you now do for me?" Let us again and again meditate on both things, especially in these times when the church in all the world awaits a time of Passion, when the whole world groans under the suffering of the political situation and is afraid of still much greater things. Let us pray to God that what he has sent us in the suffering and death of our Lord he may cause to sink so deeply into our hearts that we are able to bear the trouble that we have to bear in joyful obedience and without murmuring and falling into despair.   Amen.

VI Christ
in Despair

Crucified, dead, and buried; he descended into hell.

And about the ninth hour Jesus cried with a loud voice, "Eli, Eli, lama sabachthani?" that is, "My God, my God, why hast thou forsaken me?" (Matt. 27:46.)

THE SIGHT OF death is always something frightening. Among certain Indian tribes it is the custom that the old people, when they feel death to be near, leave their homes and look for the solitude of the wilderness in order not to defile the clean house with their death. If at all possible, people avoid those who are dying. They do not want to be reminded of the fact that this is the case with us, that our life all at once comes to this woeful and dreadful end—of dying, of being buried, dissolution, annihilation. We wish to live, not to die, and in everything we do we are determined to make our life secure and to keep death at a distance. Death is thus a true sign and indication of our creaturely weakness; in death the idea that we are "like God" vanishes. There it is "from dust to dust." The sermon of death runs, "You are nothing" —and that's what we most hate to hear.

Is it not remarkable that the picture Christianity again and again holds before our eyes is, like no other sight, the picture of One dying? It is understandable from the standpoint of the natural senses of the unbroken man when a Goethe flees the cross and when even today in an age of sports, of hygiene, and of the worship of power nothing is more despised or hated than precisely this holy picture of Christianity, the cross, the Man of Sorrows, who with a loud voice gives up the ghost. Yes, why must we always have the picture of this dying One before us? Is that not something quite morbid, contrary to nature?

But now it is not only the picture of One dying. This death has its own particular ugliness and awfulness. It is a dreadful martyr's death. Through Christian art and the custom of hearing so many beautiful things about the crucified One we have become insensitive to the fact that the crucifixion is one of the most abominable, most painful means of death that man has invented to make death as terrible as possible for the victim of his will for retribution. Only the hardest criminals were punished thus, and this punishment took place in public to frighten people. It was a public affair to torture a man to death. With the pain of death the pain of torture is connected, and with both the public exhibition that heightens both and adds shame. If the sight of a dying person is frightening, then the sight of one hanging in pain is even more so.

Jesus has really suffered death, this death, the death of torture, the criminal's death, the disgraceful death, in the presence of the whole nation. He was no Stoic who inures his soul so that it becomes as insensitive as possible to all suffering. He who is not capable of suffering is also not capable of loving. The one who is most full of love is also the one who is most capable of suffering. The more sensitively a man feels, the more frightening such a threefold pain must be for him. And yet it was not that which tormented him the most. He had to descend even deeper, there where no man could follow him with his compassion. What Jesus suffered, as he cast out the cry of pain, "Eli, Eli, lama sabachthani?" no one among us can experience. The Confession of Faith has only pointed to it with the words "descended into hell." Jesus has experienced not only the greatest human, earthly suffering; he has also suffered the tortures of hell in the literal, serious sense of the word. After his people abandoned him, his trusted ones, his disciples, also abandoned him.

It is true of course that the words, "My God, my God, why hast thou forsaken me?" is still a prayer, a call upon God. It is the word of a psalmist, at the beginning of the Twenty-second Psalm, which is a genuine song of trust. In it you read the words, "In the midst of the congregation I will praise thee," and the words, "Yea, to him shall all the proud of the earth bow down; before him shall bow all who go down to the dust." No doubt this whole psalm resounded in Jesus' soul as he raised the painful question to heaven. And yet we must take seriously his question, "Why hast thou forsaken me?" God has really abandoned him—that is the real suffering of the cross of the Savior, infinitely much deeper and more painful than all external pain of death and martyrdom and all loneliness from men. How shall we understand that and what does it have to say to us? Is it not a fact that can shake rather than strengthen our faith in him, the Redeemer and Son of God? How is it possible that the Son of God can feel himself abandoned by God?

Thus, indeed, we have to ask as long as we still have not correctly understood who Jesus Christ is and what his divine commission to us and his divine work for us is. With this "Eli, Eli, lama sabachthani?" for the first time the incarnation of God's Son has come to its goal. Therefore here also the contradiction between the gospel and all human forms of religion is consummated. It becomes evident that all religion that man himself makes has the opposite direction from that of the gospel. It is an ascent of man toward the eternal, perfect God. Up, up—that is its call. God

is high above, we are down below; and now we shall
soar by means of our moral, spiritual, and religious
endeavors out of the earthly, human depths into the
divine heights. This human religion corresponds entirely to other strivings of man. He wants to go up,
to work himself upward, to go forward, to become
happier, stronger, wiser, but also better, more pious,
more like God, and if possible, divine. Many soon lose
their breath along this high road; they cannot go
farther than striving after more happiness, more
wealth, or more pleasure. Others grasp higher; rest-
lessly they work on their education, on their ability.
Still others go farther; they strive for the highest goal,
holiness. It is almost incredible what things in the
form of privation and exertion individual men will
take upon themselves in order to reach this highest
goal. The religious history of the Indians and Jews
is rich with such truly astonishing achievements. And
yet this striving upward does not lead to the goal.
God is too high and the evil in man too deep that
man could reach the goal this way. The soul of man is
crippled or stiffened and cramped in such an ascent
to the highest height. The end is a more or less un-
confessed or unavowed despair, or a self-righteousness
that leaves room neither for genuine love of God nor
for genuine love of men. When we men wish to be
honest, then we have to say, "We cannot reach the
goal." We cannot become what we ought to become,
true men. Many let the matter rest there; they confess it, but they give in to it. They make themselves

satisfied with half because they cannot have the whole. They resign because they do not yet take God's will very seriously, before whom there can be nothing such as half achievement. God demands all, not just half. And this "all" we are not capable of giving. What is impossible for us is what God wants—all love to him and to our fellow men. "You shall love the Lord your God with all your heart, with all your soul and with all your mind" and, "you shall love your neighbor as yourself." No one has been able to do that. Therefore, along this way there is no good conscience, no trusting relationship with God, no inner peace, and no freedom of the soul.

But God has in his mercy shown us a completely different way. "Men cannot come up to me, so I will go down to them." And now God descends to us men. That is the content of the Bible, that is the gospel of Jesus Christ—the way of God to us. The good shepherd goes after his lost sheep which cannot find him by themselves. The Holy God whose commandment we can never really fulfill becomes man for our sakes in order to bring us his love which we ourselves could not reach. "God becomes man, for your sake, man." This act of becoming man begins at Christmas and ends on Good Friday. The gospel of Jesus Christ is the record of how God comes down and into the sphere of the human to bring us his divine life.

But now God does it otherwise than we would do it. He does all the work. He really goes to the end. He reaches the goal. To be sure, this end is exactly the

opposite of what we ourselves fix as a goal. We wish
to climb up to heaven; God, however, descends—
down to where? To death on the cross, says the
apostle. "He emptied himself, taking the form of
a servant, . . . humbled himself and became obedient
unto death." That is his way down to us. For our situation is indeed determined by death. We must all
die. All our exertions end with death. Finally, therefore, death gives its stamp to our life. That is why
Christ must die in order to come completely into our
condition.

· But he had to go still farther down, "to death on
the cross," to penal death. For we have all deserved
this penal death through our unfaithfulness to God.
If God would deal with us according to the law, then
we would all have to die the painful penal death that
Jesus has died. Yet even that is still not the final thing.
If God would deal with us according to the law, then
we would have to suffer not only the penal death but
also this penal death in despair, in complete separation from God, in hell. That is why Jesus Christ had
to descend into hell. He had to go the way to its very
end. There is no one here who has not deserved hell.
The rightful end of man is hell, that is, banishment
away from God—Godforsakenness. There only has
God completely come to us, there where he has taken
upon himself everything, even the cursed end of our
way. Hell we have not yet experienced. But we all
have an idea of what hell could mean. Hell is unconditional, irrevocable Godforsakenness, or uncondi-

tional despair. Something of this despair we all know, but the complete despair we have not yet experienced and we do not have to suffer it, thanks to what Jesus Christ has suffered and done for us. But we should know that he has suffered hell for us. That we should know just then when we feel ourselves near hell.

Dear friends, that is why our Lord and Savior has descended into hell, so that we do not have to live in hell. He has had to press forward to the deepest point —"Eli, Eli, lama sabachthani?"—so that we do not have to call, "My God, my God, why hast thou forsaken me?" For, when we are so troubled that we think: Now I am there in hell, now I am really in despair, now God has completely forsaken me, now I can no longer have hope, now everything is over—see, then we should hear from the cross, "Eli, Eli . . . " and know he is with us in this hell, and because he is with us, there is therefore indeed no hell. God is with me; that is why there is no longer any despair for me. Thus God has done all the work so that there is nothing in this world, not even the darkest thing, that he has not also gone through, no place in which he has not lodged. Only one thing is excepted, sin. There he never was; otherwise he would have denied himself. Indeed, he who stands completely in God's service along this path into the depths cannot all at once step out of the service of God and sin. In sin, therefore, we have no fellowship with him. There alone he is not.

But it is just there where we are in need of him so much, you say. For, when something drives us into despair, it is just then that we again and again do something evil, are disobedient, do not do God's will, transgress his commandments, make a pact with the devil, think, say, and do exactly what we should not think, say, and do. What use is all that to me about the descent of the Savior to us if he is not there with us where we have the greatest need of him? Here it is well to be careful that we do not again lose everything in the end. Jesus Christ has gone on the cross for the sake of our sin. He has not come in order to sin with you, for we really need no Savior for that—that we may find a companion in sin. Of such there are more than enough. Rather, so that you may have God for the kind of companion in sin who pulls you out of the curse of sin and redeems you from the guilt of sin. For that reason, Jesus Christ has gone into hell in order to get us out of there. For along with everything he does, that is his goal, that he may get us out, bring us to God, bind us to God, reconcile us with God, and fill us with God's Spirit. He had to despair of God for us so that we do not have to despair of God, just as he had to die the penal death so that we may become free of the punishment. He has taken all that upon himself so that we may become free of it.

Jesus has come to us and for us in hell, just as a troubled wife goes into the inn late Saturday night because she knows that she will meet there her husband who is spending his whole payday in drinking.

Truly, she does not go in to drink with her husband but to get him out of the company that is ruining him and his whole family. So the Lord has descended into hell for us in order to deliver us from it. See, just as he carries the burden of guilt for you so that you can come again to God as if you had no guilt, so he also comes into your despair so that you may know: even there he will meet with me; even that was to him not too far away from God; even there one can still be united with God through him. Jesus Christ has therefore come into everything human, even into the most terrible, so that there may be no place of man, no human experience, no difficulty, no situation, where there is no relationship with God. Everywhere he has already beforehand restored the relationship; everywhere you can call upon him, even in the deepest misery; whether it is the misery of your life, of the world, of mankind, or of the world events beyond your understanding, you can and you should know: even there the Lord Jesus is, even there he gets us out with his love.

When we speak of God's omnipresence, then we think of the omnipresence of his power. When we speak of Jesus Christ, quite particularly of the crucified One who cries, "My God, my God, why hast thou forsaken me?" then we think of the omnipresence of the divine mercy. That is what we must above all hear today in a time when despair is often so near us. Precisely that which seems at first terrible and least comforting to us, this word of pain and despair from the cross, becomes the supreme comfort and the greatest help for us. For when God is near us with his comfort, then he is also near us with his saving help which makes us new. When we really and completely let ourselves be addressed by God, "See, I am also there with you," then that is also the best help for coming out, the only help against sin, against disobedience. When I become certain that Jesus Christ is with me—then, and then alone, am I armed against evil. Then and then alone can I really do God's will. So let it then be said to you by him who has gone before you in everything: "You are in despair, behold, I have myself experienced all despair of the world." That is why you need not despair and may despair no longer. For "if God is for us, who is against us?" Amen.

VII   Easter Certainty

The third day he rose again from the dead.

Blessed be the God and Father of our Lord Jesus Christ! By his great mercy we have been born anew to a living hope through the resurrection of Jesus Christ from the dead. (I Peter 1:3.)

TWO THINGS THERE are that today determine the thinking and emotions of men: anxiety about death and hopelessness. No wonder! It is to be expected of them as of one who is surprised by bad weather upon an open field: right and left the lightning strikes; from second to second he must fear being hit and struck. The catastrophe can come upon us tomorrow; there are no safe places any longer; we are on an open field and must surrender to whatever comes. The other thing is still more evil. Namely, a feeling of complete hopelessness has come over many. There is no more justice in world history: evil triumphs; there is no more sense in living. Both these feelings indeed contradict each other, for if life is no longer worth-while, why then should one have anxiety about death? But what heart bothers itself about contradictions? It shelters both, anxiety about life and weariness of life, fearful cares about the preservation of one's life and hopelessness. Is there a means of healing this double sickness?

"Blessed be . . . God. . . . We have been born anew to a living hope through the resurrection of Jesus Christ from the dead." The Easter message is God's answer to our question. If the nations would hear it, then they should hear it as it is meant in the New Testament; then it would help them. If we this morning are really able to hear it as God's answer to our question, then it will help us.

When the apostle Peter praises God's mercy, that God has born us anew to a living hope, he is telling us that we by ourselves do not have such a living hope, that on the contrary our usual condition is one of hopelessness. Anxiety about death and a secret despair over the fact that with death everything is over is not only today but has at all times been the basic feeling of men. It comes forth very clearly today only because one can no longer hide himself very well behind all sorts of premature securities. If we keep in mind this

anxiety about death, this weird, meaningless goal of
life, many things in human existence become understandable that one could otherwise hardly understand. You know how it is when suddenly during a
theatrical performance fire breaks out, how panic
comes over the men, how they all rush to the doors,
crowding together, how one out of anxiety seeks to
hit the other with his feet and elbows for fear he could
be too late. That is a picture of human life in general; anxiety that one will be too late or that he will
come off a loser makes otherwise very good-natured
men brutal; anxiety that one could lose a place in the
sun lies at the bottom of all wars; it is the original
cause of the wild, harsh competitive struggle in business life; it makes men mutual enemies. It is anxiety
that the door will be closed, the anxiety that arises
from the thought that death is coming and that with
death everything is over.

In the world you have anxiety, says the Lord. The
world is too small for our hunger for life; anxiety is
narrowness of soul, lack of space for the soul in this
narrow, transitory world; where men have merely
this short life before them, which ends with death,
there anxiety comes over them, panic that the door
will be closed, and from this all evil and brutality.
But from this comes also vice, the seeking of pleasure,
the demand for newer and newer attractions. As one
who has anxiety that he will receive no more to eat
for a long time gulps down his food as fast as possible, so we must, when we have anxiety about death,

suck into ourselves as fast as possible the pleasures of life. Anxiety about death and the soul's hopelessness works like the vacuum of a suction pump. Were the soul filled with hope, then it would not be so greedy. Even greed stems, as does harshness, from anxiety that the door will be closed. "Let us eat and drink, for to-morrow we die."

Man is the unhappy human being who is able to think and must think beyond the moment to death and beyond that, and yet knows nothing beyond death. That is why without really knowing it his life is stamped with anxiety about death and with hope-lessness. He must always ask about the afterward and yet does not know what comes afterward or whether anything at all comes. That is his misery.

Are we, therefore, quite simply to deplore the fact that we are so unhappily created, created with the wish for eternity and yet without the certainty of eter-nity? Would we, therefore, complain to the Creator that he has so created us? Indeed, we have not set ourselves in this world in which death is the last thing, where we must therefore be anxious. And yet we notice that in this reckoning something is not right; we are anxious not because we live in the world but because we live in the world without God. That we forget God, that we reckon only with the world and not with the reality of God—this godlessness which is called sin in the Bible—this is the basis of our anxiety.

That is why this is especially great today, and in

consequence of it, also the greed for pleasure and the struggle for a place in life. The more men forget God, the more therefore does the world become the one and only thing for them—this world which ends with death—the more panic that the door will close comes over them. That is why insanity is particularly great in the world today, because forgetting God has spread widely and become common. But why do men forget God, why do they not believe in him and in his Word? Let us ask ourselves quite personally: Why do we again and again forget God? Why do we again and again reckon merely with the world and worldly things and not with God? Why do you again and again fall into this panic about the door closing and into everything that follows from panic? Because you want to be your own lord.

Indeed, men have given quite different reasons why they do not believe: the injustice in the world, doubts which come from scientific thinking, higher education, and what else? These are all evasions. I cannot believe, you say; there are too many doubts standing in the way. Quite right; but the doubts stand in the way of faith only because you will not stop being your own lord. No man has ever doubted and not believed for any other reason than this one. The will not to obey God, sin, is therefore the deepest reason for anxiety about life.

That is why anxiety cannot be overcome otherwise than by the overcoming of sin. Inseparably sin, anxiety, and hopelessness belong together on the one side, and faith, peace, and hope on the other side. We can be redeemed from hopelessness and born anew to a living hope only by being redeemed from godlessness and reconciled and united anew with God. The Easter message belongs together with the message of Good Friday. The gospel of Jesus Christ is not put together from many pieces; it is, as John very meaningfully says of the garment of Jesus, from one piece without a seam. Only he who beforehand has been reconciled to God can really believe in the Easter message, so that it becomes a living hope. One cannot deal directly with hopelessness and anxiety about death but only in such a way that one deals with the basis of it. It stems from a disturbed relation with God; it can only be removed if the relation to God is restored, if we are reconciled to God and are at peace with him through the cross of Jesus Christ. See, that is why it does not help much if one simply believes in the resurrection record of the Gospels, what one calls believing in such case. Among the many millions who have from their childhood believed and never doubted it, there are also many millions in whose life this so-called faith in the resurrection means nothing at all. Their faith is simply a piece of their world picture; they believe that Jesus is raised from the dead, as they believed that earlier lake dwellers lived in our land or that the earth is a ball. Despite this faith in the Easter event, they suffer just as others from anxiety about life, and fight, just as those who believe nothing, brutally and greedily from the door-closing panic for their place in life. Why? Just because they are not reconciled to God, because this Easter faith does not come from the experience of reconciliation with God through Jesus Christ. They have not made their peace with God; thus they also have no peace in their life. If they had peace with God, then their anxiety would also disappear, and with their anxiety the struggle for a place in life. One cannot be born again to a living hope through the resurrection of Jesus from the dead if one is not born again through Jesus Christ's act of reconciliation.

On the other hand, many say: How can I believe in the Easter message of the resurrection? I cannot know for certain whether that is true which the Gospels record; I cannot go back and prove it. And if I would simply force myself to believe it because it is recorded in the Bible—assuming that I could so force myself— how would that help me? That would not give me a joyful, living hope. They are entirely right. Such a faith whose authority is merely history has no worth. The real Easter faith does not come from the fact that one believes the report of the apostle without doubting; rather, it comes from the fact that one is reconciled to God through Jesus Christ. This reconciliation is not a mere belief but a rebirth, a new life. Through this reconciliation, godlessness and anxiety are rooted out and one becomes a new man. From this reconciliation through Jesus Christ faith in his resurrection from the dead arises of itself.

Some people have already tried to force them-

selves to believe in what the Bible reports of the resurrection of Jesus. But it was not so simple. Always
doubt interfered; and then one thought that doubt—
for example, scientific doubt in the possibility of such
a miracle—was the basis of his inability to believe.
That goes without saying. Some of the greatest scientists of all times have believed in the resurrection, just
as an apostle of early Christianity. Perhaps you also
belong to those who would like to believe, who would
also like to have this hope of eternal life. But you say
you cannot. I wish to tell you precisely why you cannot believe, and I also wish to tell you how you can
believe. You cannot believe it because you are not
reconciled to God, and you are not reconciled to God
because you do not really wish to repent for your
godlessness. All unbelief without any exception comes
from this unwillingness to obey, from the unwillingness of sin that separates us from God. In the moment
when you do that and sincerely acknowledge your
sins, then you can also believe in the reconciliation;
no, in this moment you are reconciled to God through
Jesus Christ and the truth of the Easter message is
clear to you. Then you believe in the resurrection, not
because it is reported by the apostles but because the
resurrected One himself encounters you in a living
way as he who unites you with God, as the living
Mediator. Now you yourself know it: he lives, he, the
Reconciler and Redeemer.

And now the stories of Easter become alive to you,
worthy of belief, for you now recognize in them him

who encounters you yourself. Now you believe not
only in Easter; now the Easter certainty is for you a
living experience. Now you can say with the apostle:
Blessed be the God who has born me anew to a living
hope through the resurrection of Jesus from the dead.
Were Jesus not resurrected, how could he redeem and
reconcile you? When he reconciles you to God, you
have encountered him, the resurrected One, not bod-
ily, as did the apostle, but not really any less so,
through his Word and his Spirit. Now you already
stand at the beginning of the new, eternal life. Now
you know what the Lord means when he says: "He
who believes in me has eternal life." Upon that, everything therefore depends: being reconciled to God, forgiveness of sins, removal of the separation between
you and God, joyful access to God, and peace with
God through Jesus Christ who gives you on the cross
the Father's love and with it eternal life.

Let us also look at it from the other side. One cannot say: Certainty of God, union with God, peace
with God in Jesus Christ I have, but certainty of eternal life I do not have. For I do not know what will be
after death. Of that no one knows anything certain.
See, as long as you talk so, you are not really reconciled to God, you have not experienced the living
Christ. For in the moment when he really encounters
you as the living One, in uniting you with God, you
also take part in his eternal life and the Easter message becomes a living certainty for you. As we said
before, one cannot have Easter without Good Friday;

so we must also say now, one cannot have Good Friday without Easter. For if Christ is not resurrected, how can he reconcile you with God? "If Christ is not resurrected, you are still in your sins." But if you are really reconciled to him, then you yourself have also become a witness to his resurrection.

For then you can say: "I know that my Redeemer lives." A dead person cannot be your Redeemer. When he shows himself to you as the living Presence, he speaks to you: "I live and you shall also live." He has not redeemed you in order then to allow you again to be corrupted in death; rather, he has redeemed you so that nothing, not even death, can separate you from him. When he redeems you from sin, he also redeems you from death. When he gives himself to you, he also gives you the promise and beginning of eternal life. That and nothing else is the way to the true certainty of Easter. That is why it is useless to proclaim to the world: Christ is resurrected; that you must simply believe. For the answer to this sermon is always: "The message I hear very well; only faith is lacking." The way to the faith of Easter crosses over reconciliation with God; but reconciliation with God takes place through the resurrected One who unites you with God in a living way.

But this certainty of Easter gives one's whole life a new meaning. It is foolish to say, I have no time to be bothered with eternal life, for I already have enough to do with the present. You fool, you will never be finished with the present life; you will always remain in anxiety about life and in panic until you have been reconciled to God and are certain of eternal life. But if you are reconciled to God and certain of eternal life, then you are also freed from anxiety about life and all that which follows from it. The temporal, passing life ceases to be the only important thing for you. Yes, it even ceases to be the most important thing; you notice now that it is only a preparatory school of the true life. Precisely through this, you become genuinely free to live for other men in this life and to create something genuine. The genuine joy of Easter makes men happy and loving, men who are free from the terrible panic that the door will close, the panic that makes all other men unfree, unhappy, and loveless.

But why is there so little of this new kind of life among Christians? There is no other answer at all than this: Because they are not truly reconciled to God. Because they have no genuine peace. And that means: because they have not genuinely repented or have fallen again from repentance and reconciliation. But there is no other way out of this half Christianity unworthy of belief than this: into the reconciliation, back and down to the cross of Jesus Christ! There and there alone lies the genuine joy of Easter and the certainty of Easter ready for us all.

It is therefore not true, dear friends, that eternal life is an uncertain thing. Eternal life is just as certain as the forgiveness of sins is certain for us, as we are reconciled with God. We, of course, cannot conceive of eternal life—just as we cannot conceive of God. But just as little as that hinders us from trusting and loving God, just as little does our inability to conceive of eternal life prevent the certainty and joy of hope. It suffices to know that there will be perfect life and perfect communion with God. To the degree, however, that we are certain of eternal life, we will be finished with the difficulties of this temporal life. Therefore that is the real meaning of this temporal life, that we grow into the eternal life so that this temporal life may show something of the glory of eternal life. Therefore let us shout: "Take the eternal life to which you are called!"   Amen.

VIII The Living Lord

> He ascended into heaven, and sitteth on the right hand of God the Father Almighty.

If then you have been raised with Christ, seek the things that are above, where Christ is, seated at the right hand of God. Set your minds on things that are above, not on things that are on earth. For you have died, and your life is hid with Christ in God. When Christ who is our life appears, then you also will appear with him in glory. (Col. 3:1-4.)

IN THESE FEARFUL days when small, peaceful nations have become the victims of a brutal will-to-power, the question arises in Christendom anew: Where is God? Is there no justice any longer? Can one still believe in an almighty God of love? We cannot question so. We can believe; we do not merely believe, we know, that this God who is almighty and loving is the reality above all other realities. But we also can and should ask nothing else but: Why that? What does God want that he allows all these terrible things to happen? Our text gives us the answer: Set your mind on things that are above! If we survey the history of humanity—or at least that part of humanity which one perhaps calls Christendom—over the last two or three centuries and understand its present condition as the result of this history, one thing becomes clear to us: the nations have completely forgotten to seek the things that are above. What identifies the so-called normal life of our generation is, on the contrary, a radical this-worldliness present perhaps as never before. Marxists and communists along with the bourgeois godless have reproached Christendom again and again with the charge that it preaches to the poor an otherworldliness in order to divert them from the injustices and the misery of this-world and so transform into religious devotion the feeling of indignation against the injustice that comes to them from their exploitation. Religion is the opium of the masses, they said. There may be just something in that, that the Christian hope of eternity was misused by the privileged classes. But those enemies of faith have not considered how precisely this radical this-worldliness which they preach and whose basis and goal is materialism is the strongest motive behind such unjust exploitation. The more this-worldly men become, the more violent and unscrupulous they be-

come. For if they have only the life of this-world before them, they at least want to enjoy this life as much
as possible, and in this race for the greatest possible
enjoyment and the greatest possible power the most
brutal always win; the masses of the weak, however,
become their victims. That one sees clearly enough
today precisely in the states that have made this radical this-worldliness their philosophy of state. When
they do not trouble themselves at all about an eternal
life, men allow themselves to be consumed in the
chase after the goods of this world; and this pursuit
of earthly goods as the single purpose of life makes
the individual as well as nations, in private life, in
business life as well as in politics, brutal, unscrupulous, hard, and common. This radical this-worldliness
makes every man a competitor, and so leads to conflict between all men. When even in our nation there
is so much quarreling and stench among those above
as well as those below, in the so-called good bourgeois
circles as well as among the so-called proletarian
masses, it is due to the fact that men no longer know
anything else but the earthly goods of this life, that
they seek only the things that are below. The consequence of this process of radical this-worldliness is
what we are experiencing today. "Whatever a man
sows, that he will also reap." A humanity that sows
what is below must also reap what comes from below.
That is one side of the matter. Humanity reaps today
what it has sown in the last decades and centuries.

But along with the fact that God allows all this to

come upon us, he wills something with us. He wills to awake us with it, to jolt us awake from this devastating illusion about life. Dear friends, I have, if I may think about us, the Swiss people, much more anxiety about the fact that we are again remaining exempt from the hardships that others have to go through than about the fact that we are getting into great difficulties. The worst thing that could happen to us would be that we might come through this time of cold war simply unmolested. Then we would belong, namely, to those who have in the deepest sense lost the cold war. We would not be jolted awake from what is our corruption, from the striving for only what is below. Nobody can wish that we be drawn into war; but we must for that reason pray that we shall have to participate in the general suffering at least so far that we will be jolted awake. That God wills; that is why he allows all this to happen. For mankind, it is simply necessary to experience once again in a quite terrible, evident, and grievous way how worthless all these earthly things finally are, how perishable, how hollow, how unable to give us real life; for mankind it is necessary that once again all worldly securities be taken from it so that it may learn to turn to God.

We who are here, the Christian community, should indeed not have to learn it only in this dreadful way. "If then you have been raised with Christ, seek the things that are above, where Christ is, seated at the right hand of God." The Christian community should be recognizable by the fact that its members are not like others who seek what is below, that they are not like the others who chase after the goods of this earth as if everything depended upon them, that they are not like the others who lose themselves in the world. That, Christians of all times have heard, read in the Bible, and therefore also known. But they obviously have not given others this impression. They have also taken part in this mad race and are therefore equally responsible for what has happened in our times. And every one of us, when he considers his own part, has to confess: That includes me. I, too, have not lived as one who first of all seeks the Kingdom of God and the righteousness thereof; rather, I have sunk into the world, have allowed the things that are below to capture me and have forgotten the things that are above —in spite of my Christian life. We have become worldly Christians.

Only one thing—and that is the main thing: how many of us dare affirm about ourselves that faith and hope in eternal life are the joy and strength of our present life? There are, indeed, those who like to dream of an eternal life, occupying themselves with it in their phantasy. But this disposition of this-worldliness is pure sentimentality: it does not lead to deeds; it does not therefore also make us free of worldly attachments, or free for love's service to others. Most people, however, do not think at all or do not like to think about death even though they claim to be Christians. We do not live at all, as the apostle Paul meant this and as we observe it in him as his own experience, in the joyful expectation of what lies on the other side of the threshold of death. Indeed, we believe in the eternal life, but this faith is more on the periphery than in the center of our interest; it is not the motivating power, not the enduring basis of our life. That is why we still depend much too much on the things of this-world: some on money and possessions; others on pleasures of a finer or coarser nature, on men and their opinion of us, on our favorite pursuits, on our children or our wives, on our professions, on our business or, quite simply—on this life. We cannot say with Paul: I should like to depart and be with Christ. Most of us are just as anxious about death as the others who do not believe. And now we wish to allow the word of our text to tell us what is the original cause of this condition.

Two things the apostle says, which we still remember from the church's festival days: You have died and have been raised with Christ, and your life is hid with Christ in God. To have died with Christ —that is the message of Good Friday; to have been raised with Christ, that is the message of Easter. The death of Jesus Christ is for us nothing if we have not died with him; the resurrection of our Lord is for us nothing if we have not been raised with him. Really to have heard, believed, and accepted the Good Friday message means to die with Christ; and really to have heard, believed, and accepted the Easter message means to have been raised with him. The message and this faith belong together; without this faith—that means, however, "without this dying-with and being-raised-with"—the message remains dead for us, unfruitful, a mere knowledge of the head without power in our life. And now, is it really the case that we have died with Christ? We have all indeed experienced something of what it means to repent for our sins and to seek forgiveness for them. We have all indeed experienced something of what it means that our sins are forgiven, that we may regard them as taken away through the cross of the Lord. We are no longer heathen; we believe in what has happened on Good Friday. But dare we say with the apostle that we have died with Christ? See, if that were true, then we would no longer be bound to the things of the world as we actually are. To die with Christ is to make no more claim on life but to live only from what God gives in life. We, however, are still full of claims; we still grab so much for ourselves and say: That belongs to me; that goes to me; to that I have a right; that I must have unconditionally. Thus we have only gone, as it were, to the grave of Jesus; we have not really climbed down into it, however; we are not, as it says in the letter to the Romans, buried with him. A will-to-live of our own is still there which has not yielded to God but lives completely by a power of its own. If we had really died with Christ, then there would be in us no more seeking, greediness, obstinacy, this stubborn clinging to possessions, this lack of consideration in the assertion of our worldly and spiritual claims.

There is still something unbroken in us, something that still has not come into the divine smelting furnace. There is still a part of our being that will not at all be surrendered into the death of Christ but stands on a power and will and right of its own, asserts itself and does not at all think of abdicating. This part we must uncover and carry to the cross and grave of Christ. "Those who belong to Christ," so it says in the letter to the Galatians, "have crucified the flesh with its passions and desires." The flesh, however, is nothing else than our attachment to the world. To be crucified, dead in that way, does not mean to have no more interests in the world and in what goes on in the world; rather, it means to have no longer a will of one's own but to receive everything from God and to see, will, and do everything from God's standpoint.

When that happens, so the apostle tells us, then the second thing also happens, the resurrection with Christ. For to be crucified with Christ is to know and to experience in him the One who forgives us our sins and reconciles us with God. He who, however, experiences through Jesus Christ the forgiveness of sins and reconciliation with God encounters in this way the resurrected, living, present Lord. Many have asked for years as I myself have, What does that mean, to experience the living Christ? The answer that the Scriptures give us I may pass on to you as one I am myself experiencing: We experience the living Christ when we encounter him beneath the cross as the One who reconciles us with God, through whom we receive peace with God. The cross is the place where God has condescended to be merciful to us, wills to encounter us, and where alone we can encounter him. We can encounter God only then if we ourselves descend from our high horse and pray as sinful men for forgiveness and purification. When we, however, experience there through Jesus Christ this forgiveness and this purification, he is no longer to us merely one crucified nineteen hundred years ago at Golgotha but the living, present Lord who is raised from the dead, ascended into heaven, and seated at the right hand of God. Dear friends, we can indeed only stammer these things full of mystery. Our mind is capable of grasping them only quite imperfectly, even when we reflect upon them in faith. But all that is not given to us so that we grasp it with the mind but so that it becomes a reality of life to us. "For Jesus Christ has died and been raised and become alive again that he may be Lord over the dead and the living." For this reason Jesus Christ has come into the world so that we, united with him and through him with God, "live henceforth not to ourselves but to Him who died for us and is raised." That is the new life, the life in which we no longer live by ourselves and for ourselves but by him and for him who is our Lord and Creator.

That is why it is: either we men live wrongly or live rightly. To live wrongly is to live by oneself and for oneself; to live rightly is to live by God and for

God, but also for our neighbor. Or, what is really the same: it does matter whether in our life we make ourselves lord and master or whether God is our Lord. From our standpoint we all wish, without exception, to be our own lord; the other, however, that God becomes our Lord happens only and alone through the fact that we are crucified with the crucified One and raised to new life with the resurrected One, in reconciliation with God. Only through this death of the old man can we arrive at the new, true life.

So we must understand this remarkable word of the apostle: you have died and your life is hid with Christ in God. It is through the death of the sovereign "I" that God becomes the true sovereign in us. God's lordship in us, however, is the true life, the life in which we are created, the life in and with God. Both, however, that death and this life, we can receive only through Jesus Christ, the crucified and resurrected One.

And now let us return to the beginning: "Seek the things that are above." We by ourselves cannot seek the things that are above; the weight of our sin is heavy; sinful greed always holds us chained to this world. We are sold into sin, as the Bible says, and thereby into seeking the world. We must be bought free through Christ, which happens through the fact that we die with him the crucified One and are raised with him the resurrected One. When that happens, it is meaningful to say, "Seek the things that are above"; before, it is meaningless. "If then you have been raised with Christ, seek the things that are above, where Christ is, seated at the right hand of God." Now we wish to translate that "seeking" another way: that which matters to you, you seek. Is it money or honor or pleasure or comfort that matters to you—or does it matter to you that God's will is done, that his Kingdom comes, that his name is hallowed? He who is united with Christ, to him it matters that God's and not his own will is done, that God and not he himself is honored, that God and not he himself is Lord.

And now the apostle says one last thing. When this conversion takes place within you, then you know also that death cannot get the better of you, that, rather on the other side of death the eternal glory awaits you. Take this just once as a test whether you are really united with Christ, whether to you eternal life has become a certainty, whether you have no more anxiety about death, because you think with unspeakable joy on the fact that on the other side of this world of death is the world of perfect life, your home. Perhaps you say: "Yes, sometimes that is the case with me, sometimes it is a comfort to me in the midst of all these dreadful things which are now happening that someday, indeed, the Kingdom of God and eternal life will come. But then this hope fades away and I am again anxious." See, that is a sign of the fact that you do indeed believe, that you are indeed united with Christ, but that this faith and this union are still weak. It is like a telephone connection that is there, but the electric current is too weak; one indeed hears the voice of the other, but it is weak and unclear. What does one do then? One attends to the disturbance and does not slacken until the trouble is removed and one hears the voice on the other end clearly. We have so little certainty and joy of eternal life because Christ has not truly become our Lord, and Christ has not truly become our Lord because we are not truly reconciled with God, because we do not truly want our seeking of the world to be beneath the cross. We must, as Paul expounds in the continuation of this third chapter, so to speak, slay every one of our members, not only the whole man in one lump. That is, we must hand over to Christ all our life's functions—our thinking, feeling, and willing, our imagination as well as our activity and inactivity, our sleeping and waking—so that he may forgive us and purify us, as it were one piece after another just, indeed, as one climbs into the bath as a whole man but then, however, washes and cleans one member after another. So we must hand over the whole man to Christ the Lord, but then also one thing after another, what belongs to us and what we live on, so that we may receive back from him purified the whole man, but also again one piece after another.

With all this, however, we always want to keep and should keep before our eyes the goal of all this: God's eternal goal, the glory in eternity. The more we receive the air of eternity into our soul, the more the anxiety of the world and attachment to the world disappear. The more we know ourselves as citizens and heirs of the eternal world of God, the more we shall shame ourselves for being addicted to things and for making things important that have hitherto so terribly captivated us. We must so grow into the picture of eternal life that is revealed to us through Christ that we become "disgusted ones" with what does not agree with God's Lordship. This outlook brings us under the Lordship of Christ just as, on the other hand, we have first gained this outlook through the Lordship of Christ. Let us take nothing else in the world as seriously as the promise of eternal life for all who have him as Lord—thus we shall also receive the victory over what has hitherto bound us to the things that are below. "If then you have been raised with Christ, seek the things that are above." Amen.

IX How Do We Receive
the Holy Spirit?

I believe in the Holy Ghost.

*Now when they heard this they were cut to the heart, and said
to Peter and the rest of the apostles, "Brethren, what shall we
do?" And Peter said to them, "Repent, and be baptized every
one of you in the name of Jesus Christ for the forgiveness of
your sins; and you shall receive the gift of the Holy Spirit. For
the promise is to you and to your children and to all that are
far off, every one whom the Lord our God calls to him." And
he testified with many other words and exhorted them, saying,
"Save yourselves from this crooked generation." So those who
received his word were baptized, and there were added that day
about three thousand souls.* (Acts 2:37-41.)

NO DOUBT IN these days there is much praying.
When as an individual and as a nation one sees himself standing so completely on the outside, what else

can one do to stop the torrent of calamity which, having burst from hellish depths, is discharging itself over the world?

For what are people praying? Surely most are praying that our land will be spared from war. We cannot do otherwise, and it is indeed even right to do so. Only we ourselves must be conscious of the fact that we are not helped thereby. There is still something worse than war in one's land—that is the spiritual decay of the nation. Many are praying that this time of conflicts and anxiety will come to an end; that also we cannot neglect to do, but we should still not deceive ourselves about the fact that there could be a condition of mankind that would be still more dreadful than world war. Slavery, living under a godless order, is still worse than dying. Many are praying for the victory of the just cause, therefore, that God would put an end to the lordship of doers of violence. For such a prayer we have, indeed, many models in The Psalms, so that we may and should pray thus. But suppose that the cold war comes to an end. Is it that which we have prayed for? Is thereby the corruption removed from which the cold war came? If for us Swiss so-called good or normal times were to come again—as we had it somewhat in the decades before the First World War—is it that for which we can pray to God in seriousness? Precisely in those times when everyone could seek his own profit undisturbed did not the moral level in our nation sink to the lowest point and the flight from God become most widespread? Now again it appears that we always pray first and most passionately that we shall be spared and delivered from suffering, while precisely the absence of such suffering makes us most godless, frivolous, lukewarm, and soft. We begin to despair of God as soon as things go wrong for us and others rather than when we and others become wrong. Again and again, however, God allows us not to get along well so that we learn to pay better attention to what really matters. It does not matter whether we are happy, whether we are healthy, whether we have a secure life; rather, it depends upon whether we become men, or, what means the same thing, whether God is honored in us and among us. For in the image of God we are created and are therefore really men only so far as the image of God, the love and righteousness of God, reflects from us. That is why we should pray to God that he may hammer us into shape—if necessary through misfortune, suffering, illness, loss, pain—that we become such as he planned us when he said, "Let us make man in our image." Let us not pray to God that he will spare us the difficult; rather, that he will bless to us the difficult, that he will make us right, every one of us, all Zurich and the Swiss nation, indeed the whole world. Yes, let us pray to him for blows when we have need of blows to become right.

That is why the prayer with which we can never go wrong and which will always be the most important one for this life on earth is the prayer for his Holy Spirit. For when we are driven by the Spirit of God, then we are God's sons, like him, well-pleasing to him; then and then alone are we genuine men. That is the mystery of us men, as the Bible opens it to us, that we are in need of God's Spirit, must be guided and ruled by God's Spirit, in order to become true men. Our own spirit is not given to us so that we may be our own lords through it; rather, it is given to us so that we may receive God's love, God's Holy Spirit, in it and allow ourselves to be guided by it. For this Holy Spirit of which the festival of Pentecost reminds us every year, most of all and most heartily we should pray because we have the explicit promise of fulfillment for this prayer alone. "If you then, who are evil, know how to give good gifts to your children, how much more will the heavenly Father give the Holy Spirit to those who ask him?"

Prayer, however, is only a serious thing if we are ourselves also willing to do what we can do. That is why our text is so important, because it shows us that we not only can and may pray for the Holy Spirit but that there is also something for us to do. For many, prayer is simply an escape from doing something themselves. Such prayers have no promise. The prayers of which the Holy Scriptures speak is not the calm way for those who are too lazy, too frivolous, or too cowardly to do something themselves; it is not intended to be a mountain incline that brings one to the high goal without trouble while others fatigue themselves by climbing. Prayer has a promise only if it goes together with the will to do everything that lies in our power. To the question of the people from Jerusalem whose hearts the speech of Peter had touched—the question as to what they should now do—Peter does not answer: Pray for the Holy Spirit —of course he had not forgotten the word of the Lord that commands precisely that. Rather, he points to a way that they should go, upon which the prayer for the Holy Spirit then becomes quite self-evident. "Repent, and be baptized every one of you in the name of Jesus Christ for the forgiveness of your sins; and you shall receive the gift of the Holy Spirit."

To receive the Holy Spirit and to become thereby a true man—who would not like that? At this goal we would all like to arrive if it were to be reached by mountain incline. But now it tells here where information is given to us how one may arrive at this goal—we must do something to arrive at this goal. And, indeed, what we must do is something very painful, repulsive, adverse, so that many turn away as soon as they hear it and say, "That is not for me." There is scarcely a word that is less pleasant to us than the word "repentance," "conversion." It is, however, this door to which we are stubbornly, clearly pointed in the Holy Scriptures when we ask about the way. It goes through that, and only through that; there is no other way to this goal, just as there is only this one way through the *couloir* to one particular mountain peak. If we are therefore serious enough about this to act so that we may receive the Holy Spirit and become sons of God, true men, then we must get in through here, through this *couloir,* and through no other place. We must repent.

That is why I should now like to stop preaching; I wish that God would now put such words into my mouth and so move your heart and mine that we could repent together. Yes, we should practice repentance with one another and help one another to repentance. For it is useless when one knows just exactly what repentance is, when one hears a sermon about it or reads a book about it and afterward knows more about it; rather, it all depends upon whether one repents. I wish, therefore, now only to remind us in a few words what kind of act that is, how one does it, so that we then also really do it, every one for himself. To repent is in the first place to talk with God—I should say, aloud and on one's knees in a quiet room or outside in the forest where no one will surely hear it—to talk with God just as a child talks with his father and tells him everything, what disobedient, unfaithful creatures we are. To repent is not to speak great words, but to lament to God from the heart our sorrow about ourselves, in which we tell him quite particular things that we have thought, said, and done, of which we certainly know that they are not right before him, and by which it becomes clear to us that we have a disobedient heart. Repentance is acknowledgment of sins, but such an acknowledgment that it grieves us heartily, not only that we have done that, but that we are such who could do that. To repent is to have a hearty remorse and to shame ourselves before God—before him who has done so many good things for us and whom we have rewarded with such unthankfulness. That is why repentance necessarily flows into the prayer for forgiveness of sins and for an obedient heart. Why, then, is this repentance so important? Quite simply because only so can we encounter God. As one can lay no gift in a clenched fist, so God cannot lay his love in an unrepentant heart. Repentance is the opening of the heart, that is, the whole person for God, the decramping of the heart that was previously cramped, in love with itself or gone mad about itself. To repent is really nothing else than to become honest before God and to see oneself as one is, in the mirror of God. Only when one becomes honest before God can one really receive God's word of grace. Only when one hates the disobedience in his disobedience can one be filled by the love of God. Thus we want to bow down, all the way down, with one another before God and tell him how it is with us so that he may help us to a new life.

But that we can do only because we know Jesus Christ. The people from Jerusalem had to allow themselves to be baptized in the name of Jesus Christ for the forgiveness of sins. We have already been baptized as children in this name, but this baptism is useless to us if it is not accepted in faith again and again. The baptism of children can have only this meaning: it is told to you from the beginning of your life that for you the way to God's forgiveness is opened through Jesus Christ. Baptism is like a key that someone gave us in our earliest childhood to take with us so that we might learn to use it as soon as possible, the key, namely, that opens the door to God. This key however, is of some use only to those who find the right door; but only he who repents finds the door, for one can also turn this key in other doors. But it does not open the door of God unless one has really come before this door through repentance. The forgiveness of sins—that is nothing else than free access to God. That we receive solely and alone in Jesus Christ, the one who was crucified and resurrected for us, and you receive him solely through the fact that you recognize through repentance that he has died for you, that your sins and mine made necessary this roundabout way between us and God, this horrible roundabout way which is called Golgotha.

It should really not be necessary that we repent again and again. Rather, it should be the case that once we have repented we are united with Christ and remain so henceforth. And perhaps there are even such people who do live in a continuing, unbroken bond with Christ. The rest of us, however, have experienced it to be the case, and experienced it again and again, that we free ourselves from God, go our own way, forget Christ our Lord, deny him. And then there is no other way back to him again than the one through that door to which baptism gives us the key, the way of repentance to the forgiveness of sins in Jesus Christ. If, however, it does not really grieve you that you are again disobedient, then the word "forgiveness" remains for you a mere word in your head that does not penetrate your heart and is only a concept that has no life in itself but on the contrary makes you frivolous.

The real forgiveness of sins, however, that penetrates the heart is nothing else at all than the new bond with God through Jesus Christ, free access to God, and joy in God. Have you joy in God?—then you have forgiveness of sins. Do you not know what that is, joy in God?—then you also do not know what forgiveness of sins is, then you have only the word-husk of it, the empty concept of the head, but not the reality. And that comes from the fact that you have not really repented. The way that the apostle Peter sketches is not any way for which we could substitute another one. There are not many ways leading to this goal but merely one, and he who will not go this way will never reach the goal. The way is: "Repent, and be baptized every one of you in the name of Jesus Christ for the forgiveness of sins."

But this way really leads to the goal of which we spoke at first and which all would like to reach, receiving of the Holy Spirit. For see, when it comes about that we again have access to God and rejoice in God so that a joy goes through us when the name of Jesus Christ and God is named—see, then we have the Holy Spirit. As one notices that a current is in the wire when the light bulb becomes bright with the snapping on of the switch, so one notices that the Holy Spirit is there when a joy goes through one with the naming of God's name. "Peace and joy in the Holy Spirit," says Paul. It does not always have to happen with the receiving of the Holy Spirit as strikingly as on the first Pentecost. There do not always have to be flames of fire and speaking in tongues. It can happen quite silently and unstrikingly; quite softly the door to God can open and when it opens his light flows in, without a sound and yet powerfully. Peace with God—that is the first opening of the door; joy in God—that means that it has opened wide so that, as the poet says, "your room becomes full of sun." And this opening of the door to God, that is indeed what alone matters in this life. Is the door to God open for you? Does his light in the peace and joy of the Holy Spirit really flow into your heart so you get along well even when all the world says you are getting along badly?

Peace and joy in the Holy Spirit—that is what we have need of today, what no world war can take away from us and no world peace can give us, and what is greater than all world events about which the large headlines of the newspapers report. Do not misunderstand that! There is certainly nothing small about what was being fought out on the battlefields. It is nothing small for which our soldiers were standing watch on the border, for which so many sacrifices were made. There are many beautiful things in the world that are not peace and joy in the Holy Spirit, from the gloriously blossoming apple trees and the juicy green meadows of the spring to the Swiss Confederacy and all the costly acquired freedoms of our dear fatherland; from the joyful laughing of children to Beethoven's violin concerto and Goethe's *Iphigenie*. The Holy Spirit does not want to take the place of all that and destroy it all. God's creation and the gifts of God the Creator should not be valued lowly and neglected. God does not want to separate us from all that through Jesus Christ, through repentance and faith and through the Holy Spirit. It is not true that the Christian may read nothing else besides the Bible and find nothing beautiful except the divine service. Faith and the Holy Spirit do not compete with the Creator and his gifts. Something quite different is at stake. What is at stake is: that we, who again and again misuse God's creation and the gifts of creation and forget the Creator for the creature, make the creature himself into a god; that we, who corrupt our life and our neighbor's through this misuse of creation and service of idols, become inhuman and make life inhuman; that we are freed from this inhumanity through the Holy Spirit and restored to the humanity of God's true children in whom God's creation is honored again. The Holy Spirit does not prohibit us from laughing but teaches us to laugh rightly; he wants to cauterize away the unclean from our laughing, from our enjoyment of nature, from our joy in beauty, the inhuman from our social and political life; he wants above all to remove from life what is not genuine life, as the sun kills the bacilli so that the blood may become healthy.

Perhaps many of us have already experienced a little at least how quite differently one looks at the creation of God when the joy of God and the peace of God dwell in us through the Holy Spirit. But then, of course, still another thing comes to hand: the desire for a still quite different fulfillment of the Spirit and the strong wish that what is given to us might also possibly be given to many others. "For the promise is to you and to your children and to all that are far off, every one whom the Lord our God calls to him." It is not the case with the gift of the Holy Spirit and the joy of God in one's heart, as it is for many with their beautiful little houses and little gardens: they shut themselves in and do not care any longer about what is outside. A Holy Spirit cannot be present in an egotistic encasement. A Holy Spirit is always a humane Spirit. He who has God in his heart is cognizant of the fact that he must always think of others. For he who loves God also loves God's creatures and children. Sin, evil, make one narrow-minded, ignorant, commonplace, small; God, however, makes one broad. He who finds access to God through repentance is like one who comes through a dark, narrow tunnel to Jungfraujoch: suddenly he has an immense view. He receives an interest in others who were previously of no concern to him, in his neighborhood, his city, his land, and other nations; he wishes that God's Spirit might find a path everywhere and make the life of man right. The Holy Spirit makes one not only bright but also broad. Still, it is not a general enthusiasm for humanity that brings forth great words but only seldom deeds; rather, it is that burning love which we see in our Lord Christ—"he had compassion on the people"—that does not rest until it can also do something for others. Friends, how easily all the difficult problems of present-day mankind would be solved if everywhere the Pentecost Spirit worked in the hearts of men! Why is that not the case?

You know yourself what stands in the way of the Pentecost Spirit. One does not want to change; one wants to go his own way; one does not want to repent and believe in the Lord Jesus Christ. It costs too much, it costs one's self. And when you yourself so lack the Holy Spirit, then you should not complain to God; you should not even say one must wait until God gives it. The apostle did not answer the people from Jerusalem, "Wait until it pleases God to give you the Holy Spirit." Rather, he said, "Repent and be baptized; then you will receive the gift of the Holy Spirit." Thus he also speaks to us. And when he says that, he says the other thing with it, what he received from his Lord: "Ask, and it shall be given to you; seek and you will find; knock, and it shall be opened." One cannot rightly repent without praying, and one cannot rightly pray without repenting. Both together is the only right preparation for Pentecost. Amen.

X   The Foundation
and Continuance
of the Church

I believe in . . . the holy catholic church;
the communion of saints.

*Now when Jesus came into the district of Caesarea Philippi, he
asked his disciples, "Who do men say that the Son of man is?"
And they said, "Some say John the Baptist, others say Elijah,
and others Jeremiah or one of the prophets." He said to them,
"But who do you say that I am?" Simon Peter replied, "You
are the Christ, the Son of the living God." And Jesus answered
him, "Blessed are you, Simon Bar-Jona! For flesh and blood
has not revealed this to you, but my Father who is in heaven.
And I tell you, you are Peter, and on this rock I will build my
church, and the powers of death shall not prevail against it. I
will give you the keys of the kingdom of heaven, and whatever
you bind on earth shall be bound in heaven, and whatever
you loose on earth shall be loosed in heaven." (Matt. 16:13-19.)*

THE POWERS OF death shall not prevail against it! Is there really some such thing? Even still today? Dare one say of anything in this world: that it will not be killed, that it has eternal continuance—today when everything that once seemed firm and without which we could not at all conceive the world is breaking to pieces, is being smashed and is disappearing? We are all shaken and shocked, aghast and agitated, in the innermost part of our being by the world struggle. In spite of the fact that it is something that men are doing and for which men will also have to be held responsible, it appears to us like a catastrophe of nature, a fateful, irresistible event by which all human planning and defense measures will be overwhelmed. Truly, the powers of death have overwhelmed many things. When will that come to an end?

And now it says here: one thing will never be overpowered but will remain standing throughout all catastrophes, the church of Jesus Christ, not because it is something so perfect or powerful but because it stands upon a foundation that does not waver. To speak of the church is to speak of its foundation, and to believe in its eternal continuance is to believe in him through whom and in whom it continues. About that we wish to reflect a little today, on the basis of the Scripture passage, which speaks about the first church in the New Testament and which also gives us a particularly deep insight into its nature.

"You are Peter, and on this rock I will build my church." These words, as is well known, stand in capital letters, making a huge circle in the dome of St. Peter's Church in Rome. Through a tragic misunderstanding the Roman Catholic Church has related this word of the Lord to the papacy; upon this misunderstanding, the whole Roman Church is erected, a confusion of Caesar's Roman imperialism with the Christian church. Surely nothing was farther from the Lord Jesus than such a proud organization of power that seeks spiritual ends by way of worldly diplomacy and politics and that seeks to achieve and even really achieves worldly ends by way of spiritual guidance of souls. It will always remain one of the greatest puzzles how it was possible to erect this strange and perhaps even most grandiose of all concentrations of power in history upon the gospel of the crucified Savior. The word of the Lord, which is our text, has in any case not even the slightest thing to do with that. It does not deal with the papacy and a papal church but with the fellowship of Jesus Christ, the communion of saints, which is based on the foundation of the apostles and prophets. What does our Confession of Faith mean when it says, "I believe . . . in the holy catholic church; the communion of saints"?

The word "church" is a very ambiguous, misunderstood word. One can understand by it the church building, this beautiful, medieval Fraumünster church; or one can understand by it a special polity and organization, the nature of the churches of Canton Zurich, or even the sum total of all such organizations of churches in the whole world. All that is not meant by the simple word "ecclesia" that our Lord uses here, and after him, the apostles. We would best translate it: "the fellowship of the Lord Jesus Christ," the men who with him form a living community as a body with its head, as a vine with its many different branches; the men who because they are united with him, their Heavenly Lord, also belong to one another and are dependent upon one another just as the members of a body and as the vital parts of a vine are. So the New Testament portrays the church to us. The church is not "something," neither a building nor a form of polity, neither an organization nor an institution; the church is nothing but persons, namely, human persons who are joined together through the person of their Heavenly Lord. This fellowship of men can have buildings in which they hold worship services; they can have a particular type of organization that is suitable to their purposes; they can have officers and arrangements of all kinds—but all that is not the church; rather, all that the church has. It, however, is, as the Confession of Faith says, a communion of saints; that means "men who have been seized by God and placed in his service." Our text speaks about the foundation of this church. It reports the hour of birth of the Christian church. Every Christian congregation, even the smallest and most formless, ought to regard this text as its title deed. In any case we will do so in so far as we are assembled here as the community of Jesus Christ, as the church.

The story that is told to us here begins characteris-

tically with a question: "Who do you say that I am?"
That is the first time the Lord openly asks that question. Between his questions and Peter's answer there
is a dreadful tension. What will they say? Have they
noticed it? Never has he told them. They have to
notice it for themselves; the confession, faith, has to
be their own possession. And now Peter breaks the
silence, as the one who temporarily speaks up for the
disciples. "You are the Christ, the Son of the living
God." The mystery is over; for the first time a man
knows Jesus of Nazareth to be the Christ, the promised Redeemer, the one who brings and perfects the
Kingdom of God. How was that possible? Whence
came to Peter this knowledge and certainty? It was
to him even a miracle that he knew that; he himself
did not completely understand how he came upon it.

But Jesus himself explains the mystery. "Blessed
are you, Simon Bar-Jona! For flesh and blood has not
revealed this to you, but my Father who is in heaven."
Yes, a miracle has come to pass, the greatest miracle
that can ever happen upon earth. God himself has
opened the eyes and heart of a man so he may see and
know: this man Jesus of Nazareth is the Redeemer;
in this man God himself encounters me. No human
authority, no church, no holy doctrine, no holy book,
no holy man can reveal it to him; God himself reveals
it to him; God himself allows him to participate in
his mystery. Had the Lord not said to them before,
"No one knows the Son except the Father"? Now to
this man, the fisherman Simon of Capernaum, God

himself discloses the mystery of Jesus and makes him the first Christian believer and confessor.

Up to that time men had heard about God the Creator and Lord of the world from the prophets. But God was still far away; one still could not see him in one's heart; he had given indications of the mystery of his love, forgiveness, reconciliation, and redemption, but it had still not come to pass. And now he was there, acting and speaking in one man, he himself present as the loving, saving, and forgiving God, the holy will, in Jesus the Christ. But he was there incognito, just as a king who disguises himself as a beggar and travels through his nation. Perhaps some have an idea that he is coming, perhaps one whispers to another, "Is that not the king?" until finally some one notices it and knows for sure and then speaks out: "You are the king!" So Peter noticed it because God opened his eyes and heart, and so he has expressed the awful: "You are the Messiah in whom the redeeming God is present."

In this moment the foundation stone of the Christian church is laid. For the Christian church, or let us say more clearly, the community of Jesus Christ, is there and only there where men recognize Jesus the son of the carpenter from Nazareth as their Lord and Redeemer. Everyone who recognizes that belongs to the church of Jesus Christ, and no one who does not recognize and know that belongs to the church. He may like to go to Christian worship services, he may even have been baptized, instructed, and con-

firmed, he may even honor Jesus as a particularly
holy man, as the most holy and best man that ever
lived; but if he has not recognized that Jesus is the
Redeemer, his Redeemer, then he does not yet belong
to the community of Jesus Christ. He still stands in
the entry and waits for the moment when his eyes
also shall open and he can say: "Now I also know it:
he is my Lord, before whom I unconditionally bow;
he is my Savior, whom I unconditionally trust; he is
the One in whom God sends his love and eternal life
to me. In this moment he has become a member of
the Christian community.

So it was for the first one, Peter. And that is why
the Lord says to him, "Blessed are you, Simon Bar-
Jona!" and then continues to say, "You are Peter, and
on this rock I will build my church." From that time
on the fisherman Simon has the name Cephas, or
Peter, which means "rock." This title of honor he
has held because he was the first confessor of Christ,
the foundation stone of the church.

Upon the confession of Jesus Christ the church is
built, as the confession on its side rests upon the witness of God's Spirit in the inner man. To everyone for
whom God opens the heart for Jesus the Christ the
duty is now given to speak out loudly what he has
recognized in the inner man. There are many who
think that one should lock the decisively religious in
the inner man. There is something right in that,
namely, a holy terror of making the Most Holy idle
talk. Talk is so cheap, pious words come so easily; but

to recognize Christ as one's Lord is surely the opposite of something that is cheap and easy. That is why one should not make it idle talk. But confession is something different from talk; confession is a public obligation. He who confesses Jesus Christ is now publicly obligated to take seriously the Lordship of Christ. Otherwise, he turns out to be simply a hypocrite.

One should not really take so lightly the confession of Jesus Christ, as the church has unfortunately done so often and down to this day. One ought to know that it is a powerful thing when a man publicly confesses: I belong to this Christ, my Lord. Confession is a kind of oath to the flag; one pledges unconditional loyalty to the Lord. One is obligated to stand by him at any cost and to submit to him; one is obligated to give him unconditional, blind obedience and unconditional blind trust. Confession of faith is an unconditional declaration of loyalty, an oath of allegiance. Upon this confession the Christian community rests. After Peter came the other apostles; after the apostles, the three thousand on Whitsunday and then the expansion of the community throughout the whole world. All of them had to be ready at any time to be imprisoned, tormented, and killed for the sake of their oath of loyalty, their confession of this Lord, and many of them have paid this price from the first days of the Christian community on.

But Peter is not only the first confessor. As such he would not be the rock upon which Jesus wills to build his community. Rather, Peter is the apostle, that is, the ambassador of God, whose witness to Jesus Christ awakens faith in other men. Not Peter as a person but his function as an apostle is the foundation of the church. We can see that all apostles stand together in the early church; Peter, of course, is the leading figure among them, the speaker and organizer in their midst. Never is it his person, however, upon which the authority rests but upon the apostolic office that was conferred upon him and the other ten. Upon this apostolic office the whole church rests because we would have no proclamation of Jesus Christ without the apostles. To them the mystery was first entrusted; only they as the first ones could, and had to, pass it on. Just because they as the first have this distinction, there is no continuation of the apostolic office. It was something once for all just as the revelation of God in Jesus Christ himself, just as the cross and the resurrection, were something once for all. This foundation was laid once for all; it never has to be laid again. Jesus Christ, as he is proclaimed and handed down to us through the words of the apostles, is the foundation of the church.

So also the words about the keys to the Kingdom of God are to be understood. The community of Jesus Christ is a holy temple. No one can enter this temple by himself. Only he who has been invited can enter. He is invited, however, by the forgiving love of God in Jesus Christ. This word of reconciliation is entrusted to the apostles and to Peter as the first. He for whom he opens the temple with these keys, that is, he who believes in Jesus Christ as Savior through the word of reconciliation, enters the temple and becomes a member of the community of Christ; but everyone who takes offense at this word of reconciliation remains outside. To him who says yes to Jesus Christ on earth—we know now what this "yes" means; it is the "yes" of trust and obedience—yes is said in heaven, in eternity. And to him who says no to Jesus Christ on earth no is said in heaven, in eternity. That is the decision before which every man is placed.

That is the decision before which also every one of us is placed. Do you say yes to the God who comes to you in Jesus Christ as your Lord and Savior? Or are you and do you want to continue to be your own lord and savior? Do you see that with all the power and cleverness which you have—you cannot save yourself from corruption—or do you still believe that every one is the maker of his own fortune? Dear friends, human self-confidence has been given a hard jolt in our times. Many have for the first time noticed what empty phrases these words are: self-confidence, self-reliance, the power of the nation, our dignity. The man who puts his trust in himself is fantastic. He may be an able man at his post, but one day there comes a time when he has reached the end and when he must see that he has played the wrong cards. Granted, it is not easy for a powerful, brave, and clever man to understand how this could ever possibly happen to him. But if he is really honest with himself, he must see it and will see it. If he takes God's commandments seriously, he must see that he does not obey them and therefore needs forgiveness and redemption. If he does not evade the meaninglessness of death, he must see how futile this life is if there is not an eternal completion, and that he cannot make this but can only receive it. It is important to see that what the New Testament calls love is the real meaning of life, and that we ourselves do not have precisely this love and cannot give it to ourselves but can only receive it. He who sees that is ripe to recognize Jesus Christ as his Lord and Redeemer. In this moment, when this recognition breaks through into him, he belongs to the community of Jesus Christ.

And now let us return to the beginning. Of this church the Lord says: because it is built upon this rock, the powers of death cannot prevail against it. He who through Jesus Christ has found and won fellowship with the living God does not perish in death. To take part in Christ means to take part in eternal life, in the resurrection and in the perfection of all things, in the Kingdom of God. He who belongs to Christ belongs to him in eternity. When God binds himself to someone, he does not bind himself just for a time but forever. It is good that these evil and dangerous times have again brought us closer to the vision of eternity. We had miserably fallen in love with the temporal, with this world. He who is entangled in the temporal can, however, not give his best here, for behind everything lurks that fear that he will lose the temporal. Only he who is certain of eternal life is free of the fear of death. And only he who is free from the fear of death is truly strong and free. That is the first thing: eternal life is promised to him who believes in Jesus Christ.

The second thing, however, is this, that also the church as a whole has a part in the promise of eternal life. Not only every individual Christian but also the community of Christ is destined for eternity. "The individual Christian" is really a misunderstanding; there is no such thing. Just as there cannot be an individual hand or an individual arm—it is then cut off and dead—so there cannot be an individual Christian. A Christian is always a member of the community or he is no Christian. This community of Christ, however, is the only one upon earth to which is promised imperishableness. All others will sooner or later pass away; every state, every race, every culture, every work of art has its time—perhaps long, perhaps short—but someday it will no longer exist just as someday we will no longer exist. But one thing will never cease to be, the community of Jesus Christ, the church that is built upon Peter's rock. I do not mean the so-called Catholic Church, not even the Reformed Church, but the community of those who belong to Jesus Christ through trust, obedience, and loyalty. To them a beginning of eternal life is already given here; and this eternal life cannot die, rather, it has the promise of eternal life. That is the powerful confidence which the church has. It may be

attacked, hated, mocked, oppressed; its organization
may be destroyed, its activities may be extremely con-
fined—yet it remains and will outlive everything else
that is great and lasting.

For the church is the true community, the community founded upon God's love. It is the only community that is not built upon an egotistic motive. All
other communities, from the most intimate friend-
ship to the most inclusive national community, con-
tain an egotistic element; one wants to have something from it for himself. The Christian community
alone is, if it is what it ought to be, free from that. It
is unconditional love for the other, that love which
God alone can give and which he gives us through
Jesus Christ and his Holy Spirit.

That is why this fellowship is also the salt of every
national community. There is just so much true and
lasting community in our nation as there is Christian
fellowship, the church of Jesus Christ, in it. The ruin
of the church is the ruin of the nation; the decline
of the churches is also the decline of real national
unity. It is not civilization and culture, nor blood and
soil, that can really unite us but only love, disinter-
ested, sacrificing, selfless love—that love which Jesus
Christ alone gives us. That is what will teach and
show us God in these stormy times. He shakes everything so we will see what will really stand forever. He
takes many things away from us so we will at last grasp
what has eternal worth. He shakes even our nation
so it will find its way back to the community that will

never cease to be because it rests upon rocky ground, because it is descended from the Spirit of God himself. I believe in the holy catholic church, the communion of saints, because it is nothing else but the community of God's love founded on Jesus Christ himself. We belong to this communion of saints if we allow ourselves to be seized by this love of God, and we are part of the indestructible church if we remain in it in faith's trust and obedience.   Amen.

XI Judgment and Forgiveness

I believe in . . . the forgiveness of sins.

If thou, O Lord, shouldst mark iniquities,
Lord, who could stand?
But there is forgiveness with thee,
that thou mayest be feared. (Ps. 130:3-4.)

WHO WILL STAND? Who has stood? A storm has gone over the world and is going still farther over us all. What will it leave standing? We cannot see anything other than a judgment of God in this storm, a judgment upon our whole godless and therefore rootless modern culture and civilization. God often uses for his judgments very strange instruments. The godless Assyrians and Babylonians he used in order to execute upon his people judgment which the prophets had long before foretold. Even to these nations a turn would eventually come; but at first they were in all their insolence and God-despising nature his executioners of judgment. So he used one hundred and fifty years ago a Napoleon to pulverize a decayed and rotten political system in Europe—until then the day came when God's scourges were themselves crushed. So God is also working today "in the wild storm" and letting it become obvious how hollow was much of what seemed great and strong. Even we shall not be spared this test-judgment. What will stand? So much is certain: either our nation will stand, we will let ourselves be called to consciousness and repentance, to turning away from a materialistic and egotistic understanding of life toward God and his righteousness; or we will go under and deserve to go under. No nation can in the long run live off the sacrifices that earlier generations have made. If the sense of sacrifice dies, if awe in the face of God's commandments dies, then things are ripe for going under. This question is now placed before us: Will you Swiss people be able to take upon yourselves the heaviest sacrifice for your independence, or will you sell your freedom for economic profit and material prosperity? What will be more valuable to you, to have it good for a while as before, at the price of independence, or to draw the belt tighter, to renounce, to get through narrowly, to do without, in order to save independence and honor? How shall we stand this test? And who will stand it?

Our text speaks, however, not of this test and of this standing. The word of Schiller that world history is world judgment is only a half-truth. There are judgments of God in world history, that is true; and that we are experiencing today. But all these judgments which we experience here upon earth are only preludes to the Great Judgment that will come at the end of the times for us all, for every one of us when he steps off this world stage and is called over the threshold to eternity. Then every one of us must come before God's face; then the Holy God stands as judge before him. Then you yourself must answer for everything you have done and unfortunately not done, said and unfortunately not said, thought and unfortunately not thought. Then you will be weighed on God's scales. That is the most serious thought we can think.

Let me say something about seriousness. Often old people say to young people: "Boy, girl, you do not yet know how serious life is." Perhaps they themselves do not know what is serious. They think the seriousness of life is that all kinds of difficulties befall one, that there are many disappointments and many hardships about which youth have no idea. But that is not serious; that is perhaps sad or dangerous or miserable. But the fact alone that we are held responsible is serious. We have read these days in the newspapers from a neighboring country: The guilty will be held inexorably responsible. That is serious. Seriousness is there where we have responsibility, where we are held responsible in the final all-inclusive sense.

The most serious question, the only unconditionally serious question is therefore this: How shall we stand that test? Dear friends, every one of us is completely different from the other, and the life of every one is different from every other one. For no one up to now has it gone, or will it ever go, just the same as for the other. As the faces of all are different—all the millions of faces of human beings—so also the courses of life are different. But one thing is the same among us all, quite exactly the same: we shall all eventually die, and we shall all be placed before the judgment seat of God in the Last Judgment, in the Final Judgment, the unbelievers and the believers, those who scoffed at the idea of a judgment and those who already knew that what the Scriptures say is true. How will we then stand when we shall stand before God's face?

And now the pious poet of Ps. 130 tells us: in this judgment no one could stand if God wished to charge sins to his account. Therefore, a third thing that is the same for us all: not only must we all die, we must all appear before God's judgment seat; but also, we cannot stand in this judgment if sins are charged to us. Why not? Because we are all sinners. That you know; first of all, one's conscience tells one that, and secondly, one has by this time often heard it in sermons or read it in the Bible. And that is why it no longer makes a strong impression. Yes, we are all "chief sinners." We do not stand in the judgment if God marks our iniquities, even that we have known for a long time. But now the dreadful happens: we skip joyfully over this most serious of all thoughts with comfort—God does not mark our iniquities; he forgives us our sins. That, too, one has often heard from his youth. The word "forgiveness" is like a lightning rod that allows us to remain calm even during the greatest thunderstorm. Nothing matters, the lightning will not strike us, for indeed we have a lightning rod! The judgment of God will do nothing to us: we are Christians; we believe indeed in the forgiveness of sins. We joke somewhat about those who go to confession to receive absolution there—that means precisely forgiveness of sins—and then, since the burden is taken away from them, joyfully free from it sin again, knowing that they can go there again one day and unload. We are right when we rebel against that; but we do not often notice that we who know the word "forgiveness" of sins as well as those often do quite the same thing at bottom as they, only that a priest does not bestow absolution upon us, but we ourselves. "I know I have sinned—but God forgives. I know that I cannot stand before God's judgment if he should mark iniquities. But he is indeed merciful and does not mark iniquities but forgives us our sins out of his wonderful goodness. *Summa summarum:* it is not bad; the matter is not so serious as it seemed at first. In the first part of the sermon the preacher speaks of sins and powerfully arouses one, and in the second part of the sermon he speaks of the forgiveness of sins and then cheers one up again. We know that by this time and that is why we no longer take even the first part of the sermon as dreadfully serious; we know just how it finally comes out." One is like a curious reader who first reads the ending of the story and knows that the hero is still alive at the end, and then one needs no longer be afraid for him, even when one reads about the worst dangers into which he comes. We know, indeed, the happy ending. So our Christianity is for many—and probably for every one of us at times—just such a happy-ending story in which we know that it will not come out so badly because God ultimately forgives sins.

See, there we are running across one of the rottenest points in our whole Christianity, and this rottenness in Christianity is perhaps one of the main causes of what one could call the European rottenness. If the Christian community, which should still be the salt of the earth, has already begun to rot to such an extent because of this unseriousness, then how will the more or less unbelieving, heathen world learn something of true seriousness from us? We have made something out of one of the greatest, holiest words of the Bible, out of the word "forgiveness," that is not at all in its meaning but runs exactly counter to it.

For that, however, the Bible is not really responsible. For it tells us clearly enough that one dare not go such a circuitous way with forgiveness. Thus the psalmist tells us: "But there is forgiveness with thee, that thou mayest be feared." Where fear of God is gone, there faith is that salt-become-tasteless which is good for nothing, so that one may throw it away and let it be trampled down by people. Dear friends, what terrible kinds of mountains of salt-become-tasteless Christianity has heaped up! How much of this unserious Christianity is in your life and mine! What a misuse of the word "forgiveness" we have encouraged, namely, that it does not lead us to the fear of God but has made us heedless and filled us with that false lightning-rod optimism. How many have we preachers already involved in guilt with us through a false sermon about forgiveness! I do not like to think of the moment when God will present me with the bill for all the wrong things that may have gone forth from my way of preaching the forgiveness of sins. Every sermon is false, indeed godless, that does not lead those who hear it to repentance, does not fill them with a true, holy awe before God. Every so-called evangelical comfort, every comfort from the cross of Jesus Christ, is a false, indeed a cursed, comfort that is merely pleasant without at the same time being dead serious. I have often asked myself precisely in these weeks whether it would not perhaps be good if just once for a time nothing more would be said about the forgiveness of sins but instead of that we would speak quite simply about the judgment of God, about the fact that we are all called to an accounting by God and must answer ourselves for everything before him. Not because the sermon about forgiveness would not be true; it is and remains the dearest page of the Bible, and the word "forgiveness" of sins is and remains the greatest, holiest, and costliest word that we know; but because nothing is so bad as the frivolous use of this holiest and costliest word and its dulling effect upon the conscience if it is not closely protected from misuse.

What does the psalmist mean when he says, "There is forgiveness with thee, that thou mayest be feared"? He wants to tell us in the first place: forgiveness is something that one cannot have unless one receives it with God himself doing it. Forgiveness is no article of merchandise that one can obtain from God just as one could in earlier times obtain an indulgence paper from a priest with money. Forgiveness is only for those to have who subject themselves humbly before God. For forgiveness is the sovereign act of grace of the divine King. Just as one who is sentenced by the court has only one way out—to appeal to the grace of the supreme government of the country that it may grant him grace rather than law—so forgiveness is the last possibility that the Holy God alone has to absolve us from his judgment. Only he who acknowledges this regal majesty of God, only he who subjects himself awfully before the sentence of His judgment, has any prospect that God may make use of his law of grace toward him.

See, that is why Jesus our Savior, the Son of God, has been slain for us on the cross, that we do not come to a cheap forgiveness. Between us and forgiveness now stands the cross on Golgotha. There the word of the psalmist is fulfilled: "There is forgiveness with thee, that thou mayest be feared." For there God our Holy Lord tells us that he cannot and will not simply shove aside our sin and our sins as if they were nothing, but that it cost him infinitely much, that it has cost him the life of his Son. The severe judgment of God is not simply put away, laid away, but it is carried out and worked out on him, the un-guilty One, so that we can be saved. Yes, it is true, "God does not will the death of the sinner but that he returns to him." It is true: that God loves us his creatures, infinitely and incomprehensibly, in spite of all our disloyalty, our frivolity, and our defiance; that we may and should believe when we are in de-spair over ourselves and think there is no longer any salvation, that we are lost since we cannot, indeed, stand in the court of God. But that is something other than cheap forgiveness. God does not pass over our sins; he goes through them when he forgives us in Jesus Christ and calls us his dear children.

That is also why we should not simply pass over our sin to forgiveness, but should go through the cross of Jesus Christ. We should know how much it has cost him so that he can nevertheless accept us and call us to himself. Yes, even more: we must take upon our-selves the judgment that there the Son of God suffers, and say: "I am really the one judged; the punishing hand of God was meant for *me* as it struck him, the righteous One, on the cross. *I* deserve the wrath that he has taken. I, the sinner, was judged and slain there so that I can live as God's child." Only through this judgment of God, through this fire, in which all my sinful desires, my self-will, my frivolity, my feelings of hate, my self-seeking are destroyed, can I obtain the forgiveness of God. I must fear God the Judge if I would rightly love God the merciful Father. I must, therefore, renounce all that is contrary to God in my life if I would enjoy his love.

Let us say it quite simply: there is no forgiveness of sins without a truly repentant heart to which sin is sincerely painful and which renounces it with all its power and in all honesty. To wish to have God's forgiveness without this renunciation of things contrary to God, that is crazy frivolity; that is to carry on a mischievous game with the grace of God. Certainly, God anticipates us. He has not waited until it is painful for us; he does not say, "First I want to see your repentance, then I will show you my forgiveness." He is not like a cautious tradesman who first wants to see your purchasing money before he gives up his costly goods. God goes beforehand in incomprehensible love and mercy: he does everything first; he shows us his grace first; he himself, he quite alone, pays our whole bill of debts. But he has done all that in such a way that we shall lay hold of his mercy and can experience it in no other way than through penitence and repentance. To him only He gives his forgiveness who says to Jesus Christ: "O Lord, what you suffered is all my burden; I, I, am guilty of what you have borne." He who says that honestly repents; for him, it is grievous; he returns, he renounces what is not right, he shames himself for what he has done wrong and hates in himself the things that contravene God. He says to God: "I dare and will no longer be the one who I was, for you, Lord, have made me new in Christ." Another one, however, who wishes to have it cheaper, will not fall to his share. He can, indeed, catch a momentary semblance of comfort so that it again becomes for him a little lighter. In reality he has not received forgiveness; rather, he has only forgiven himself. And that is why this comfort of forgiveness does not really make one joyful, does not give peace to one's heart, does not create fellowship with God, and therefore also has no fruit of love along with it.

That is why it is that forgiveness is no article of merchandise that we can obtain from God but fellowship with God—a re-presented, restored relationship between us the creatures and him the Creator. "There is forgiveness with thee, that thou mayest be feared"—that we now understand. For if one is really united with God, then one also has fear of God, awe before the Holy God, a holy respect for his orders and commandments. When a child is related to his mother in a genuine, affectionate love, then it does not say: "I may do that. Mother has forbidden it but she is a dear mother—she will let me get away with it." A child who thinks so does not really love his mother; and a mother who would behave so with her child would not be a true mother but a sentimental person who does not deserve to have a child. A genuine relationship between a mother and a child is such that the child receives through it a fear of doing anything that the mother does not like.

So much more is a genuine relationship with the God who is not only merciful but also holy, not only gracious but also just, always a willingness to obey him and a fear of doing anything that is not right before him. Where this fear and this willingness is not there, the relationship is also not there; then, however, forgiveness of sins is also not there. For forgiveness of sins is, indeed, not alone and not, above all, the setting aside of guilt but the new relationship with God, the joyful relationship of God's children, the certainty that nothing can separate me from the love of God. The obedience and willingness to do good that comes from such a relationship is a much stronger safeguard against evil than the fear of punishment. For stronger than fear is love; love of God, however, includes in it the fear of God, awe before the Almighty Creator and the Holy Lord.

It is the mystery of the divine wisdom and love to reveal itself to us in the cross of Jesus Christ and to give us his forgiving mercy in such a way that it can only be received by a willingly obedient heart. Of course one can also misunderstand the cross of Christ, so that it becomes a cover of sins instead of a power against sin. But let us have no illusions about that: one cannot receive forgiveness thus but merely a deceiving semblance of it. One can have indulgence cheaply and continue to sin freely, but not forgiveness. Genuine, true forgiveness is the most effective means against sin, against all evil. For all evil comes from awelessness and lovelessness. Forgiveness, however, is the receiving of the holy love of God. He who does not wish to love God, and therefore to obey him, again falls immediately away from forgiveness.

That does not mean that one may become a sinless saint through forgiveness and whoever is not one therefore has no part in forgiveness. Then we would all be lost; then we would fall into sin again and again. But he who really lives in the real forgiveness of God through Jesus Christ, in him is a power against sin that does not allow him to sin freely but gives him power against it and, when he has fallen again, immediately reminds and reprimands him and disgusts him with sin. For even we, we who are certain of the forgiveness of God in Jesus Christ, will indeed appear before the judgment seat of Christ and have to give an accounting about everything. There it will then appear whether we have really stood in the forgiveness or merely played with forgiveness and deceived ourselves and others. This seriousness remains with us; but if we are really united with God through Christ, it is no seriousness that frightens us or lets us despair but a seriousness that warns us to remain in it and not wantonly to risk the gift. So the fear of God must remain the root of our faith and the joyful, childlike love of God, its crown. Amen.

XII I Am
the Resurrection

I believe in . . . the resurrection of the
body; and the life everlasting.

*I am the resurrection and the life; he who believes in me,
though he die, yet shall he live.* (John 11:25.)

WE HAVE THOUGHT recently more about dying
and about death than ever before. Many of us at the
beginning of the last war looked upon our lives as finished, and since then take every day we still live as a
special gift of God. But another question is
whether we were really prepared for death. In those
days of panic even Christians lost their heads because
they had a terrible anxiety about death. Anxiety about
death is for us men the natural thing, but not for us
Christians. For a Christian is, indeed, one who be-

lieves what the Lord says to us in our text today: "I am the resurrection and the life; he who believes in me, though he die, yet shall he live." In this anxiety it appears that we have not yet or not yet rightly learned to set our sight on eternal life as the goal that we are going to meet with longing and hope.

Let us speak frankly with one another about this. We present-day Christians have allowed ourselves to be infected with the this-worldly spirit of the time. Of course we have not joined the radical emancipation from faith in the other world; most Christians believe somehow that there is a life after death, that the soul is immortal, that with death everything is not over, or what are similar figures of speech. But we have still allowed ourselves to be influenced by the modern contempt for otherworldly Christianity and, above all, with the others have bestowed our main interest on the things of this-world to such a degree that for the otherworldly things only a little interest remains. We have made a kind of compromise with the modern worshipers of this-world and despisers of the other world by thinking in some such way: This visible, earthly world is still God's creation: one should not condemn it as a valley of tears; it is really the miracle work of God. And this earthly life is the life that God gives us, which it is our task to develop. Here is our place of work, the vineyard in which the Lord calls and places us. Here family and native land, vocation and human duty, demand our whole attention. Here are the neighbors whom we ought to love;

whether we have been true to the realization of the talents entrusted to us will be decided when once we are called to give an accounting. Therefore we must, so long as this life still lasts, give our whole attention to it and can confidently allow what awaits us on the other side of death's line to come upon us when it comes. Is it not true that we have taken just about such a position to this question?

But now we see in the New Testament a completely different attitude. The Christian community is directly fulfilled by this one thing: by the coming eternal world, by the hope and certainty of the resurrection. As a prize-runner races toward his goal, so the Christian community races toward this coming eternal world which has penetrated its heart and determined its outlook. The whole message of the New Testament is concerned with the future of the Lord Jesus and with the coming of his Kingdom. Of course it does not think of a world somewhere above or beneath this earth but of a breaking of an eternal world into this world. It does not pray: "Make me pious so that I may enter heaven." But it does pray: "Thy kingdom come." But the Kingdom for whose coming it prays is the Kingdom of the resurrection and of eternal life, the life that knows no more of death, suffering, perishableness, and contradictions, life in the perfection of God and his love. This hope for an eternal life is for the first Christians not something about which they like to think when they are old, not a comforting prize for those who no longer have anything for which to hope in this real, earthly life. On the contrary the expectation of this eternal life is everything to them. Who is Jesus for them? He is the Messiah, which means the one who brings the sovereignty of God and the resurrection. What are they primarily thinking of when they thank God for the coming of Christ? They are thanking him primarily because he has given them in Jesus Christ certainty of eternal life and access to it. The expectation of the resurrection, of the return of Jesus, of judgment and perfection, is not a part, nor the last and most unimportant part, of their Christian faith; rather, it is the quintessence; it is the sap and kernel of their Christian faith. One can say plainly: A Christian is a man who through Jesus Christ hopes for eternal life.

How monstrously sharp and clear is the contrast with what we have just now observed to be the attitude and outlook of the average Christian today! We can see in this contrast what kind of mixture of modern this-worldliness and Christian hope is our ordinary Christianity.

But now the unveilings that God has allowed to happen in this modern world come to us to help bring us through once again to the Biblical, Christian hope. A glance at the events in our time can make it clear to us whither the this-worldly orientation of life leads. One says: Here on earth we are to love men as our neighbors, not in some other world. Quite right, here alone are they whom we ought to help and to whom we ought to do good. Thereupon the Bible does not leave any doubt. But how does one come to love this neighbor? Here is the great fallacy of modern men. They think: The less one thinks about another world, the more one will love his neighbor. The Bible tells us the opposite, and the experience of our century confirms it. It is even understandable when one meditates upon it more deeply. The less men have a hope beyond this life, the more they will ruin themselves with pleasures and goods, the more greedily do they grasp in this short time for the things that they can get possession of, the more materialistic and egotistic they become.

Or one other thing. Let us ask: When have marriage and the family been held more sacred, then among the first Christians as the New Testament shows us or in the modern world that is completely this-worldly? Once again contrary to our first impression we must say: then when men hoped and waited for eternity, marriage and the family received the stamp of holiness. The sense of the holy, awe, disappears to the extent that the hope for eternal life fades. The man who has nothing to fear and hope for on the other side of death loses that sense of what is holy and unholy, respect for God's unimpeachable orders.

One more example. Who serves his country most faithfully and most disinterestedly, he for whom this earthly life is the principle thing or he who as the apostle Paul says of himself and the other Christians: "Our commonwealth is in heaven, and from it we await a Savior, the Lord Jesus Christ"? Again the answer is completely contrary to what seems obvious: He who has been freed most from the earthly world will serve most faithfully and most disinterestedly his home and his fellow citizens. The more certain of eternal life and the more desirous of the Kingdom of God a man is, the more distance he puts between himself and what otherwise imprisons men, the more free he is for service.

But we do not need this proof from experience if we would bow obediently before the divine word. Our Lord Christ speaks: "I am the resurrection and the life; he who believes in me, though he die, yet shall he live." Thus he says: You have no idea who I am and what I mean for you, have done and will do for you, if you do not look beyond this life to eternity. He is no human peacemaker, no political messiah or savior. Earthly messiahs we have enough of today and can see just what they can do. We already have an idea what the end of all this will be—an end with terror. Jesus, however, says to us: If you want to understand me, you must go beyond the temporal to the eternal, for I am he who brings the Kingdom of God to you, that through me you may win entrance into eternal life. He who will not do that should keep his hands off me and my gospel. To men who are satisfied with the world and the things of the world I will have nothing—nothing at all—to say except this: that they must go to their own ruin. But to those who have noticed that this earthly life in itself has no meaning but can receive its meaning only from beyond, to them I say: I guarantee you this goal; yes, even more: I am this goal. I am the resurrection and the life.

Is it not true that that is difficult to understand? How can Christ be my goal? How can he himself be the resurrection, my resurrection and the resurrection of all believers? And yet it is so because Jesus Christ is not only a man but because he is the one in whom God calls us to himself, reveals himself to us and offers us his life as the fulfillment of all our hopes. "I am the resurrection and the life," he alone can say who may say: "I and the father are one." But we must venture to say it even more boldly when we really want to understand what Christ means here: You man, whoever you are, man or woman, high or low, you have from God one meaning and one goal of your life. You shall not remain what you are, but you will become what Christ is. For he is the fulfiller and the ideal of human nature. You shall not only become as he is, but you shall take part in him, in his own divine-human nature. To live in him in eternity —that is the true eternal life, that is the fulfillment of human destiny, the destiny of all men, at least of all those who reach their destiny. From eternity we are destined through Jesus Christ to receive in the Son of God divine, eternal life and in this to find our fulfillment, our true human nature. He, Christ, is sent to us by God to awaken us to eternal life from the nothingness of death into which all of us have sunk.

How, dear friends, can we know that that is true?

What can we say against those who tell us that no one knows what will be on the other side, not even you? You should say to him: You are right, I know as little as you. But God knows and God has revealed it to me in Jesus Christ his Son. To believe in him—and that I do as a Christian—means, therefore, to be certain of this, his promise. One cannot believe in Jesus Christ without at the same time believing in this promise of his. It is one with him himself. For "I am the resurrection and the life," he says. And now he continues: "He who believes in me, though he die, yet shall he live." Certainty of our eternal life is for us by all means based upon faith in Jesus Christ. There may still be other reasons why we may believe in a beyond, in a continuation of life after death or perhaps in the immortality of the soul. But all these are weak and uncertain, even illusory. Many will answer: Even the ground Jesus Christ upon which you stand is weak and illusory. One will say that so long as he does not know what this faith is and how it arises. One cannot simply one beautiful day decide to believe in him, and then by this faith be assured of eternal life. That would be an all too cheap thing, because the Bible tells us that faith is a costly thing, a costly pearl that costs no less than all. What does it mean to believe in Jesus Christ? It is simple to say: I believe that he is the Son of God, as it is written in the Bible, and I believe that he is the Redeemer, as it is written in the Bible and as the church teaches us. But all that is not the kind of faith of which the Bible itself speaks. To believe in him means much more there: through him to repent, to be brought to a complete conversion; and through him, through complete trust in him and complete obedience to Him, to become a new man.

The Bible uses for that the strongest expressions there are: You must die with Christ the crucified One, and you must be resurrected with Christ the resurrected One. You as the old, willful, self-seeking, prideful, godless man must die. This, your own will, must be broken; your pride, your conceit about your own existence and ability must be destroyed. And when you have ceased to trust in yourself, then you must put your trust in him as your helper and Redeemer, as the One whom God has given to you in order to bind you with him and to re-create you in him. Only he who believes in this way may also say: though I die, yet shall I live, for Christ is my resurrection and my life.

Dear friends—the most certain thing we know about our future is that we must die, and that therefore our life and everything that makes life worthwhile for us will be destroyed. No beautiful words can change that. Death is the end. The question is whether there is beyond this end still a hope greater than everything that this earth has to give us. This hope the gospel of Jesus Christ alone offers us, every one of us. But it offers us it at a price: the price is that we believe in him. To believe in him, however, means quite simply to be his disciple. If you will be his disciple, then take and receive what he promises you. If you really want to be his disciple, then there is no difficulty in receiving this. The difficulty lies only in whether you really want to be his disciple, whether you want to renounce your own rights and will. If that happens, then henceforth you know: He is my resurrection and my life.   Amen.